Reprint Publishing

For People Who Go For Originals.

www.reprintpublishing.com

Dogs Pointing Quail.

ROB AND HIS GUN

BY

WILLIAM ALEXANDER LINN

ILLUSTRATED

NEW YORK
CHARLES SCRIBNER'S SONS
1902

COPYRIGHT, 1902, BY
CHARLES SCRIBNER'S SONS

Published, September, 1902

TROW DIRECTORY
PRINTING AND BOOKBINDING COMPANY
NEW YORK

PREFACE

THE author hopes that this book will be found by its young readers both interesting and instructive. Its object is to introduce them to some of the pleasures of country life, and to give them practical hints of the methods by which they may become expert with the gun and rifle, make them acquainted with game of different kinds and the manner of hunting it, and at the same time point out to them the difference between the pleasure of a true sportsman and the taking of life for the mere sake of killing.

It may add to the interest in Rob's experiences to know that the narrative is a description of actual hunting expeditions of the author, and that the incidents related and the persons described have come under his personal observation.

CONTENTS

CHAPTER I

PAGE

COUSIN DAVE'S VISIT TO THE CITY 1

    Meeting with Rob in Madison Square—Discussion of the Boy's Future—Boyhood Memories Recalled—The Story of the Capture of a Big Rabbit—Some Questions and Answers.

CHAPTER II

LEARNING ABOUT THINGS 14

    Rob's First Morning at the Farm—Introduction to the Dogs—Pointers and Setters—Something about Dog-Training—Trying for a Point—Rob's First Sight of a Rabbit—Bird-Lore.

CHAPTER III

A FIRST LESSON IN SHOOTING 24

    Advantages of Modern Appliances—Fitting Rob with a Gun—A Clay-Pigeon Trap and its Use—Some Things a True Sportsman Should Remember—Rob's Introduction to Wing-Shooting—Its Primary Difficulties—A Hit at Last—A Present of a Dog—Hints about Handling Bird-Dogs.

CONTENTS

CHAPTER IV

PAGE

A September Walk 36

Lessons in Farm-Work—An Interesting Experience with a Woodcock—How it Tried to Protect its Young—Summer and Fall Shooting Compared—Looking for Quail with the Dogs—Flushing a Partridge—Putting Rob to a Test—Trailing and Winding—A Talk about Ruffed Grouse and a Sight of One on the Ground.

CHAPTER V

Rob's First Day's Hunt 53

A Find of Quail—Necessity of Picking out One's Bird—A Double Miss—Better Work Next Time—Sport with Fall Woodcock—Rob Gets a Rabbit—A Lost Flock of Quail—More Woodcock, and a Beautiful Exhibition by Tass—One of Cousin Dave's Recollections—Trying for Partridges—A Good Retrieve—Something about Aiming.

CHAPTER VI

Shooting Bay-Snipe 73

Varieties and Habits of the Birds—An Early Breakfast and a Sail—The Blind and Stools—The Art of Whistling—A First Shot and Others after it—Whistling under Difficulties—Willets and Sickle-Bills.

CONTENTS

CHAPTER VII

A TRIP TO THE ADIRONDACKS 92

 Welcome at the Home-Camp—Its Comfort and Equipment—Off for a Deer-Hunt—Crossing a Carry—A Row down Raquette River—Making a Camp in the Woods—The First Day's Hunt and its Disappointment—A Capture of Ducks—How Rob Got his First Deer—A Day's Tramp in the Woods—Seeing a Bear—An Exhibition of Partridges—A Deer in the Distance.

CHAPTER VIII

DUCK-SHOOTING ON BARNEGAT BAY 117

 Jesse and His Yacht—Living in Close Quarters—The Sneak-Box and its Uses—Jesse as a Cook—Hiding in the Open Bay—Putting out the Decoys—A Shot at Broad-Bills—Rob's Good Marksmanship—Cousin Dave's Goose Story—A Poor Day for Ducks, but Some Good Luck with Brant.

CHAPTER IX

QUAIL-SHOOTING IN NORTH CAROLINA 144

 An Introduction to Mose—What an Early Start Means in the South—Good Work of the Dogs—Beginning of a Fine Bag—Lunching on Persimmons—Mose as a Preacher—Joe's Long Point—A Lucky Find.

CONTENTS

CHAPTER X

PAGE

IN THE CANADA BUSH 160

A Tiresome Trip and Some Poor Quarters—A Long Wait for a Team—Accommodations in the Bush, with a Dinner of Salt Pork—A Beautiful View of Deer that was also an Aggravation—Venison at Last—A Still Hunt in the Snow—How Rob Killed a Doe—After a Big Buck—Rob's Shot from an Island—Antlers to be Proud of.

CHAPTER XI

WILD-GOOSE SHOOTING IN DAKOTA 189

Rob's First View of the Prairie—A Hunting Outfit on the Plains—A Night in the Open, with Some Nasal Music—About Goose Pits and Decoys—A Morning Disappointment but a Big Afternoon's Sport—Attractions and Excitements of Goose-Shooting—How Mr. Aileen Escaped from a Bear—A Shot at Prairie-Chickens.

ILLUSTRATIONS

	FACING PAGE
Dogs Pointing Quail	*Frontispiece*
Cousin Dave's Farm	14
Woodcock — Ruffed Grouse — Quail	38
Bay-Snipe Shooting	80
Home Camp in the Adirondacks	94
Duck-Shooting on Barnegat Bay	132
Cap Delivering a Retrieved Quail	158
Shooting Wild Geese in Dakota	200

ROB AND HIS GUN

CHAPTER I

COUSIN DAVE'S VISIT TO THE CITY

ON one of those bright afternoons in the latter part of March which give New Yorkers a foretaste of the real spring which is approaching, there might have been noticed among the persons who were sauntering through Madison Square a tall and well-built man, whose tanned face and general appearance would class him as a visitor from the country. He seemed interested in the occupants of the benches, in the children who were exercising on their roller skates, and in the men who were at work in the park. Before two of these who were putting one of the beds in order he stopped, and watched their labors with an attention that might have been interpreted as indicating some knowledge of his own on the subject of flower-gardening, and a willingness to learn more. While thus occupied, one of the older lads on skates glided up to him, and, grasping him by the arm, said, in a tone of pleased surprise,

"Why, Cousin Dave!"

The man so addressed replied, "Why, Cousin Rob."

"What are you doing in Madison Square?" asked the boy. "Are you going to make us a visit?"

"Some business brought me to the city, and I did think I would spend the night with you if it is convenient."

"Convenient," exclaimed the boy; "of course it will be convenient, and papa will be delighted to see you."

"All right," said Cousin Dave; "finish your skating, and I will go to the house with you."

"I have skated enough," said Rob. "We will go at once. Shall we walk?"

"By all means; I am a countryman, you know, and the city sights are a novelty to me."

So they walked up Fifth Avenue together, the boy pointing out the well-known houses to his cousin, and the man enjoying the sight of the pedestrians on the sidewalk, the vehicles and fine horses on the roadway, and the buildings that lined it. A short distance below Central Park they turned into a side street and were soon at Rob's home.

Now, a word of introduction to these people whom we have met, and with whom we are to become better acquainted. Cousin Dave was David Warren, and Rob was Robert Edsall. Mr. Warren was a cousin also of Rob's father, Thomas Edsall, and therefore a second cousin to Rob. Thomas and David had been boys, and country boys, together. Living on adjoining farms, they had attended the same school and enjoyed the same sports, until they had become young men. Then Thomas entered a counting-room in the city, and became a successful man of business. He found that this success in itself made growing demands on his time, and for many years he had not had an opportunity to revisit the old country region wherein his boyhood had been passed. But its memory had not failed him, and the occasional visits of his Cousin David to the city had afforded him opportunity to live over again, in their conversations, the boy's experiences that he had enjoyed so well.

No announcement, therefore, could have given him greater pleasure than Rob's greeting, when he came home that evening, "O, papa, who do you think is here? Cousin Dave."

One of the old-time talks, of course, occupied the evening, and in the course of it Rob became the subject of discussion.

"What are you going to make of your boy?" asked David.

"That is a matter that I have tried to keep in the background," replied his father. "Rob is a good student, and I think a bright one. I have a theory that the most important thing to discover, in deciding a boy's career, is what he *wants* to be. I think it is Ruskin who holds to the doctrine that a man who can succeed in one walk of life can in any other. I would not go quite so far as that, but I do concede the folly of trying to drive a boy into some occupation for which he has a distaste."

"Is the boy rugged?" queried David. "It seemed to me that he had a delicate look, but my country eye may not be the best judge of a city constitution."

"I would not call him delicate, but he has his

mother's constitution, not mine, and he has not had the benefit of that country life which did so much toward giving me the strength to do what I have since done. In fact, Rob knows very little about the country. He was born here, has been educated here, and his vacations have been spent with his mother at Newport, where I do not think the real life of the country exists."

"Do you know what I would do with that boy if he were mine?" asked David.

"No," said his father, "but I am interested to hear."

"I would send him to the country to live with his Cousin Dave till he got tired of the life."

"But his studies, Dave! He is almost prepared for college, and to send him to the country now would be to put him back indefinitely."

"If you are going to make a college-man and a professional man of him, my advice would be unwise. But I would not make such a future for him. I judge horses and dogs a good deal by inspiration, and I apply the same test sometimes to men and boys. And if I am any judge of Rob, he has in him a liking for things rural that would require very little cultivation for full development. A good deal is said, and said truly, about the damage to agriculture that is done by the drift of the best of the farmers' boys to the towns and cities. Why should not some of this damage be offset by taking some of the bright city boys to the country, inculcating in them a love for country life and activities, and giving agriculture the benefit of their intelligence?"

"Do you seriously propose to me to make Rob a farmer?"

"Well, I'll tell you candidly, Tom, I don't think Rob is a very strongly built lad, and if he does need a tonic there is none that will do him the good that will come from farm life and farm air. At any rate, think over the idea of sending him to me for his summer vacation. If he does not get too homesick, and likes the occupations I shall plan for him, it will be time enough to discuss something more permanent."

Mrs. Edsall joined them at this time, and the subject was discussed further by the three. Neither parent showed a great inclination toward the idea of making the boy a farmer, but both did accept the

COUSIN DAVE'S VISIT TO THE CITY

invitation for the vacation, and there the matter rested for the night.

To Mr. Warren Rob did look actually delicate, and, having taken a liking to him in his former visits, he felt a great desire to give the boy the benefit of that country tonic in which he had so much faith. Accordingly, at the breakfast-table the next morning, he turned the conversation in a direction which would enable him to form some idea of his younger cousin's tastes.

"Tom," he remarked, "do you ever hunt any more?"

"Hunt?" was the reply. "I have not shot off a gun in twenty years."

"And yet you used to like it as much as I did."

"Like it? I like it yet, but I have no time, or perhaps I ought to say no opportunity."

"Well, I'd take time," continued David, "and you know a real sportsman must find his opportunity."

"Why, papa," Rob queried, "did you ever hunt with a gun?"

"Yes," his father replied, "with a gun, when I could get one, and before that with a bow and arrow, or an old pistol."

Cousin Dave began to laugh. "Do you remember, Tom, the day we got the big rabbit out of Farmer Martin's stone fence?"

"As if it was yesterday."

"O, Cousin Dave, do tell me about it!" exclaimed Rob.

David looked significantly toward his elder cousin, indicating his acceptance of the boy's interest in the subject as evidence of the correctness of his surmise about the boy's tastes, and said:

"Boys begin to track rabbits long before they can hope to shoot birds———"

"How can they track rabbits, and why can they not shoot birds at the same time?" interrupted Rob.

"As to the rabbits, boys can track them because a rabbit makes a track that is different from the track of any other of the wild animals, like this"—and he made a sketch of a rabbit's track on the cloth with the handle of his knife—two dots, side by side, and two at right angles to them in the rear. "When a country boy sees this track in the snow he knows that only a rabbit has made it, and the two hind tracks act as a guide to the direction which the rabbit has taken. As to your other question, boys shoot, or catch, rabbits before they can shoot birds, because the true sportsman shoots only game-birds, and only shoots these on the wing, and it requires long practice to be what is called a 'wing shot.' Now for my story. One morning, in early December, when your father and I woke up (he had spent the night with me, as he did a good many nights), we found the ground covered with a light coating of snow, and the sky clear. This was an ideal condition for rabbit tracking, if the snow had not continued to fall till morning. Rabbits feed at night, and if the snow had fallen till daylight their tracks of the night before would have been covered up. The hired man told us that it had not snowed after midnight, and we had no doubt, therefore, of some success. I remember that I wanted to take 'Gyp,' the old bird-dog——"

"What is a bird-dog?" asked Rob.

Again Cousin Dave smiled. "A bird-dog is a dog that, by its nature and training, is able to track game by scenting it, and point it when it is found."

"How point it?" again asked Rob.

"When a good bird-dog comes near to the game it stops, stretches its neck toward the game and stiffens its tail. Don't you remember, in 'Pickwick,' how the action of a bird-dog puzzled Mr. Winkle?"

"Yes, I do," said Rob, who was a great lover of Dickens, "but I never just understood what it all meant."

"Now, Rob," said his father, "let your cousin finish his story, or the snow will all be melted before we get to the rabbit-ground."

"'Gyp' stayed home on this occasion, your father insisting that, with so good a snow, we should have no use for a dog. But the snow was lighter than we had expected to find it, and where the weeds were tall no tracks could be seen. We had been told to be home for dinner, and at eleven o'clock we had not secured a rabbit. The sun had come out warm, and on the sunny side of the fences not a particle of the snow was left. We had turned our footsteps homeward, and about decided that we were 'skunked,' when a stone, thrown by your father into a brushheap, started out one of the biggest rabbits I had ever seen. We had only one gun between us, and that was in my hands. If ever a boy had an attack of buck-fever over a rabbit——"

"What is 'buck-fever'?" Rob again interrupted to ask.

"The sight of a man's first deer (and sometimes of his second and third) is always supposed to excite him so much that it becomes impossible for him to shoot at all, or, if he fires, to hit the deer. This excitement sportsmen call 'buck-fever.' I had it sure, and, seeing the rabbit jumping toward a pair of bars which would take it on the other side of a stone fence, I fired both barrels of my gun, without taking aim, and so without touching it. Your father, who had observed what a big rabbit it was, scolded me roundly for letting it escape, and I was ashamed of myself. However, I now had an opportunity of scolding him, and telling him that if we had brought the dog we could have tracked the rabbit and had another shot. 'Well, come on,' he said, 'perhaps there's snow enough the other side of this fence to track it after all.' This proved to be the case. The snow still lay on the shady side of the fence, and in it were the big tracks of our escaped game. We were rabbit-wise enough to know that the rabbit would probably soon turn into the fence, and so it did, its tracks giving away its retreat. But now another obstacle confronted us. The place in the fence where the rabbit lay concealed was not two hundred yards from the house of a farmer who thought he had no bigger enemy than a boy ready to pull a hole in one of his fences to catch a rabbit. If he caught us we were likely to get a hiding. But that big rabbit was worth some risk. So, while your father kept watch on the farm-house, I pulled out a few stones, and there sat the rabbit within reach of my hand. I soon had him by the ears, and then, stooping down to keep within shelter of the fence, we ran for home as fast as we could."

"What did you do with the rabbit?" asked Rob.

"We killed it and had it for dinner the next day. It was the only rabbit I ever killed that weighed seven pounds. What would you have done with it?"

"I think," said Rob, "I would have given it another chance to run away, and redeemed my marksmanship."

"That is a very sportsmanlike reply," said Cousin Dave, "but we did not take any chances."

Cousin Dave left the city that afternoon, but the seed he had sown took root. Rob's father and mother talked over Mr. Warren's proposition, and

COUSIN DAVE'S VISIT TO THE CITY

Rob was never so well entertained as when he could get his father into the library of an evening and induce him to tell stories of his early experiences with dog and gun. A few weeks later the boy took a severe cold, and, when he was able to go about the house again, the family physician suggested the advisability of giving him the benefit of country air. Thus it came about that one May evening found Rob at his cousin's farm.

CHAPTER II

LEARNING ABOUT THINGS

ROB was sound asleep the next morning when he heard a knock at his door and the cheery voice of Cousin Dave calling, "Breakfast." He was soon dressed, and out in the yard, where he found his cousin attending to some of the morning chores.

If a boy has any innate love for the country it will display itself on such a morning as that on which Rob made his acquaintance with his cousin's farm. The sun was bright, the air agreeably cool, and the landscape was decked in its freshest garb. The young foliage on the trees looked as soft as velvet, and the meadows and pasture-fields were carpeted with a lovely green. The farm-house was shaded by big maples, and into a tank near the kitchen door a stream of spring-water was bubbling. Off to the left the land ascended in natural terraces to the top of a mountain, and from the piazza could be seen stretches of sward, interspersed with the bright leaves

Cousin Dave's Farm.

LEARNING ABOUT THINGS

of peach and apple orchards, from which the blossoms had not yet fallen.

"I am so glad you called me," said Rob, "as I want to see the cows milked."

Cousin Dave gave one of his hearty laughs. "Now the joke is on you," said he. "The cows have been milked for an hour, and are out in the field."

Rob was amazed to find that farm-work began at so early an hour, and asked why he was not called sooner. His cousin assured him that he could in future set his own hours, but explained that he had let him sleep because he thought he must be tired after his journey of the day before.

They soon went in to breakfast, and there Rob discovered some of the differences between city and country ways. All sat down to the table together; there was no waiter to pass the dishes, and everyone did his or her part in handing what was asked for. Rob was amazed at the size of the pieces of bread, and at the huge pile on the plate, and wondered why his Cousin Annie, who was the house-keeper, cut so much. But this was changed to another wonder when he saw how rapidly the pile disappeared, and had to be replaced.

After breakfast Rob and Mr. Warren went out into the yard, and the latter asked, "Now, what should you like to see first?"

"I think," said Rob, "I should like to see a bird-dog."

"Jim," called Mr. Warren to one of the men, "let out the dogs."

In a moment there was heard a great barking from behind the shed, and four beautiful dogs came racing up to Mr. Warren, apparently ready to leap upon him. He had only to raise his hand, however, to make them desist, and they were satisfied to be called by their names and to receive a stroke of his hand.

"O!" exclaimed Rob, "have you so many dogs?"

His cousin then gave him his first lesson in dog-lore. He explained that the two dogs with a shaggy coat were setters, and those with a short, sleek coat were pointers. These names were given them, he said, not because the dogs indicated the presence of game in a different way, but simply to distinguish the species. Some sportsmen preferred one kind, and some another. Pointers were said to be the more easily broken, but he had not found this to be

LEARNING ABOUT THINGS

a rule. The pointers, with their short coats, were cleaner dogs than the long-haired setters, and in hunting in the South, where there are a great many burs, the setters' coats often got so full of them that they could scarcely travel.

Then Rob was told the dogs' names: the two setters were Czar and Tass, and the pointers were Cap and Dan.

"What did you mean by a dog's being broken?" asked the boy.

"Broken simply means trained. While a well-bred dog has the sense of smell highly developed, and by his nature stops when he gets close to the game, there are many things which he has to be taught to make him of the most use in the field. For instance, he must know, to begin with, that he *must* mind. What I tell a dog to do he *must* do at once. Of course a hunting-dog is not asked by a good master to do what is against his nature, but there are a great many things that come to him almost naturally when they are pointed out to him. For instance, we do not want the dogs to begin hunting until we come to the place where we expect to find game. If they did they would tire themselves out unnecessarily. So one of the first things they are taught is to 'heel'—that is, to keep behind their master when he wants them to. I will let you see how they do this. But first I will show you another of their elementary lessons. A dog must always lie down when he is told to. The command to lie down is the word 'charge.'"

Raising his hand, their master said, in a commanding tone, "Charge," and every dog crouched down on the ground. Then, stepping forward, he called Czar, and Czar leaped forward. He let him run in front of him a little way, and then called out, "Czar, heel." The obedient dog at once came back and followed behind his master's steps.

"O, Cousin Dave," exclaimed Rob, "is it not wonderful?"

"Only as an exhibition of what intelligence in the dog and patience in the master can accomplish. I consider dog-training a gift. Some men have a gift in teaching birds and animals, and I do not think that a man who does not really love a dog can be a good teacher of one."

"Who taught yours?" asked Rob.

"I always break my own dogs, but many sports-

LEARNING ABOUT THINGS

men, including all who live in cities, could not do this, even if they had the skill and patience. But I think a dog always works best for the man who has shown him what he is to do."

"And what else do bird-dogs have to learn?"

"O, you have only seen them at their a, b, c's. This is the closed season for game (I will explain about that later), but I may be able to let you see some other results of their education."

Sending three of the dogs back to their kennels, they went with Czar into a field near by, where the unploughed stubble afforded some cover. Mr. Warren said that they might be able to find a rabbit sitting in his resting-place, or, more likely, a meadow-lark in the grass. Czar was kept "to heel" until they were well out in the field. Then his master cried, "Hie on," and away he bounded, eager for the sport. Rob noticed at once that the dog did not run forward in a straight line, but zigzagged across the field. "That," his cousin explained, "is what is meant by 'ranging.' If the dog ran straight across the field he would discover no game that did not lie right in front of him. But he is taught to 'range,' that is, cover the whole field as he runs through it. The value of a quail-dog depends in a large degree on his being a good ranger."

"There goes a bird!" cried Rob.

"Notice it carefully. Do you see anything peculiar in its flight?"

"No—o," said Rob, doubtfully.

"That is because you have still to take your lessons in bird-lore. Almost every species of bird has a flight of its own, and a countryman ought to be able to distinguish any bird, as far as he can see it distinctly, simply by its manner of flight. That bird was a meadow-lark, and if you will notice closely the next one that gets up you will see that it flies first with a sort of sailing motion, and then with a flicker of its wings. Even if its color did not distinguish it, you could tell it from its flight."

This seemed very wonderful to Rob, and he confessed to himself that he feared he would have to take a great many lessons before he could thus tell one bird from another.

As they walked along, Mr. Warren explained that trained dogs would not point small birds, like sparrows, and that the law did not permit the shooting of meadow-larks. But these birds had a game scent,

LEARNING ABOUT THINGS

and, while he would not encourage a young dog to point them, it would do no harm to an old dog like Czar to have a little practice with them.

Other larks now got up, but far ahead of them. When Czar approached a part of the field where the stubble was taller he moved more carefully, his tail wagged vigorously, and then he stopped and stood as rigid as a statue.

"O," exclaimed Rob, "Cousin Dave, is that a point?"

"Yes, that is a point."

"And how long will he stand there?"

"It would be hard to tell. Czar is an old dog, and what we call a 'stanch' one—that is, one who will keep his point until told to break it. While he is standing there I may tell you that some dogs are trained to put up (technically, to 'flush') the bird when the hunter is ready to shoot. Others will not break their point even at the command. I think it best to let a dog stand while the hunter puts up the bird if the animal can only be driven from his point. But it is very convenient sometimes to let the dog flush the game, especially if it lies in thick cover. All my dogs are trained to do so."

They had now approached quite near the old dog, and could see the eager look with which he was apparently trying to fix his eye on what was in front of him. After letting Rob enjoy the sight a few moments, Mr. Warren said, "Now we will see what there is there. It may be that the bird has risen, and that he only catches the scent it has left behind. This sometimes occurs, and meadow-larks are a wary bird, and in thin cover do not lie well. Hie on, Czar."

Czar moved forward, and out of the grass went, not a bird, but a big rabbit.

It was just as much Czar's nature to chase that rabbit as it would have been if he had been only a common dog, but his master cried, "Drop," and down he went on his belly.

Rob's enthusiasm was aroused to the highest point. Was the rabbit, he asked, as big a one as his father and cousin had tracked into the stone wall? Could they have shot it if they had had a gun? Would Czar be able to point it again? To the latter query his cousin replied that the rabbit would probably find some hole in the ground, or in a fence, where it would be safe for the present. He also explained

LEARNING ABOUT THINGS

that rabbits were not considered very highly as game by sportsmen, and that some dogs were not allowed to point them, although this was something that few dogs would learn. When they were hunted it was usually with a hound, a dog that has a " good nose," that is, a keen scent, but routs and follows the game instead of pointing it. A good hound would run a rabbit quite slowly, and the rabbit, in doubling on its own track, would generally come back near the starting point, and thus be within reach of the hunter's gun.

We have not time to follow Rob in all his lessons in dog and bird lore, and must content ourselves with the information that he did, before the summer was over, acquire skill in distinguishing the common birds by their flight, spent many hours with his cousin studying birds with the aid of an opera-glass, and found his enjoyment of country-life increased a hundred-fold by the knowledge he thus obtained. It was a favorite saying of Mr. Warren's that the country resident who does not know the birds and the flowers that are seen on every hand, loses one of the greatest attractions of his surroundings.

CHAPTER III

A FIRST LESSON IN SHOOTING

AFTER dinner of the first day (they dined at noon at the farm), Mr. Warren asked Rob to follow him upstairs as he wanted to show him his "gun-room." This Rob found to be a small chamber which was devoted to guns and other shooting paraphernalia. All these were explained to Rob in due order. He was taught the difference between the muzzle-loaders, which, his cousin said, were the only guns in use when Rob's father and he were boys, and the modern breech-loader. He was shown the empty paper-shells and the loading tools, and told what an advantage smokeless powder was in the field and the uses of different sizes of shot. He handled guns of different weight, and found no difficulty in understanding the superiority of a heavy gun in shooting ducks from a boat, and the advantage of a light one in tramping all day over the field.

A FIRST LESSON IN SHOOTING

"Yes," remarked Mr. Warren, "things in the shooting line have changed wonderfully since your father and I were boys. It would seem slow work now, loading a gun every time it was necessary, with a ramrod. I remember, by the way, getting so excited once when a boy in hurrying to load my gun to shoot a squirrel out of a tree-top that I shot away my ramrod. And with smokeless powder it is very easy to mark the birds of a flock as they fly away, whereas, with the black powder, we often had to kneel down to look under the smoke, in order to mark the birds, and even to see if our shot had taken effect. And yet I am not sure that the new inventions have not been a disadvantage to good sport. It is a mathematical certainty that, the more game is shot, the less there will be left, and breech-loaders and smokeless powder do help kill off the birds. This is especially noticeable with the bay birds and wild fowl, which had a fair chance when a hunter had to spend some minutes, standing up, in reloading his gun, but which stand a poor show when a gun can be reloaded instantly, and without exposing the shooter. However, everyone wants the best that's made, and so it is with the sportsman, and the man who does not use the best will be distanced."

After this bit of philosophizing, Mr. Warren took down a light twelve-gauge gun, of a well-known make, and asked Rob to level it and see how he thought it would suit him. Rob did not exactly know what a gun should be to "suit him," but his cousin explained that it should adjust itself naturally to his shoulder, without requiring two or three efforts to get it there, and that the stock should be so bent that the holder of the weapon could sight it at once. After several lessons in bringing it up and sighting it, under Mr. Warren's direction, Rob decided (or perhaps it would be more correct to say that Mr. Warren decided for him) that the gun was a good fit, except that the stock wanted a very little shortening, which could be easily effected. Then Rob was told that this gun was to be his, and a very proud boy he was when he carried it to his own room, to make its better acquaintance, as his cousin suggested. The latter did not give him any cartridges to go with it, wisely deciding that the first use of cartridges ought to be made under his own eye.

A FIRST LESSON IN SHOOTING

One of Rob's first questions the next morning was, "Cousin Dave, how can a boy learn to shoot?"

"Practice is the principal thing. But the very best shots—I mean wing-shots—have a natural gift, which is born in them. I do not say that a boy who has not this gift cannot become a good shot, but if he has the gift he will be saved lots of trouble and many a disappointment."

"Then, if I want practice, how can I get it when the season for all kinds of game is 'closed,' as you called it yesterday morning?"

"The season is called 'closed' when the law forbids the killing of a certain kind of game. This law is enacted to preserve what game we have left. Game laws are not always very wisely drawn, but they all aim to forbid the shooting in the early spring and throughout the breeding season. Game laws differ in different States, and the open seasons for different kind of game are different. For instance, in this State it is lawful to shoot woodcock in July, while quail and ruffed grouse (called in the Northern States partridge) can be shot only in November and December. This is because the woodcock hatches its young very early in the spring, and they are supposed to be big enough to eat in July. There is a growing prejudice, however, against this summer shooting, for one reason, because there are men who will shoot quail in July as soon as woodcock if they put them up. I carry too much flesh to find pleasure in tramping through a miry swamp under a July sun, in the hope of killing a few birds that are not strong enough to give themselves a fair chance to escape. But I have got away from your question about practice-shooting. I think the first practice I will give you will be over a trap with clay pigeons."

"I am afraid I don't understand those terms," said Rob.

"Of course not. Come out to the wagon-shed and I'll show you."

There, Rob was first shown a trap. This was a sort of spring arrangement, and the "clay pigeon" was not a bird at all, but a clay saucer. When the trap was set, and the so-called pigeon placed in it, the pulling of a cord sprung the trap, and away sailed the clay "bird" with a pretty good imitation of the flight of a real one.

"I don't say," Mr. Warren explained, "that a

A FIRST LESSON IN SHOOTING

clay bird out of a trap is as good a practice-mark as a real bird. But, in the first place, no real sportsman, and no good-hearted boy, would shoot our song-birds just for practice. And, in the second place, while many sportsmen do shoot tame pigeons which are let out of a trap, I am opposed to taking life in this way, and to leaving wounded birds to die, as many of them certainly will. Be a true sportsman, Rob, from the start. Never kill anything just for the sake of killing. Shoot no more game birds, no matter how abundant they are, than your reasonable wants for food require. Give every wild thing you hunt, whether it be a bird or a deer, a chance for its life. If you follow these rules, you need not feel very badly if some tender-hearted young lady chides you for shooting game under any circumstances."

Later, in the afternoon, when Mr. Warren had attended to some of the details of his farm work, one of the men carried the trap into a field, and Rob had his first experience in marksmanship. Mr. Warren stood behind the trap first, and showed him how to hold his gun, when to give the order " pull," and how to aim. It did look so very easy to break those "birds" as they sailed away in front of the marksman, and when four had been shattered to pieces at the explosion of Mr. Warren's gun, Rob did have a feeling that he would surprise his cousin.

So he stepped into place with some confidence when he was told to, got his gun in position, as his cousin directed, and said "pull." Then something occurred that he had not counted on. The mark that seemed to fly so quietly and smoothly when Mr. Warren was at the trap, now appeared to the boy to be rushing away from him at a speed that required the utmost quickness on his part to fire his gun at all before the bird disappeared on the ground, to say nothing of taking any aim. So there came two "bang" "bangs" before his gun was fairly at his shoulder, and the merriest kind of a laugh from Cousin Dave.

"Kill 'em both?" asked the latter.

"I did not see but one," replied Rob.

"Did you see that one?"

"Not very long. Don't they go like a streak?"

"You think they do. The first feeling of a young wing-shot is that the game is going to get away from him, and that he must fire just as quickly as possible or lose it. Whereas, the fact is that, if he does

A FIRST LESSON IN SHOOTING

slam-bang without aim, he is going to score a miss, sure. Try it again, and promise not to fire until I cry 'shoot.'"

Again the trap was set, and again Rob took his place. He was now told to bring his gun up several times before the word "pull" was given, in the way of practice. Then a clay bird was placed in the trap, and the string was pulled. "Wait," cried Cousin Dave, "till I say shoot." But he did not say the word, and the mark sailed to the ground without being shot at. "Did you follow it?" Rob was asked. Yes, he thought he did. "I did that," it was explained to him, "to get you used to taking aim. Now, we will have another bird." Rob gave the word "pull" this time, and again he missed. "Only what I expected," was the encouraging comment of his instructor. "If you had hit it, it would have been little else than an accident. You see, you have everything to learn."

Mr. Warren now fired four times, missing one of the shots, to Rob's encouragement, for the boy regarded him as invincible, and then Rob took his place again.

"Now," said Mr. Warren, "you are going to break

this one. The trap is fixed to throw the bird very straight up into the air, and I want you to shoot just when it has reached the highest point. There, for a moment, it is stationary."

When Rob fired, the clay saucer was broken into a hundred pieces. " I pealed it," cried Rob, in great delight.

" I guess you did. Took all the skin off it. Don't think that bird would make even pot-pie."

This practice was continued for an hour, during which Rob broke several more of the birds, missing more than he broke, of course, but gaining confidence in himself, and becoming a little accustomed to the handling of the gun and the rapid flight of the marks.

Thus, Rob had his first lesson in wing-shooting.

As they walked back to the house, Mr. Warren said: " Along with your lessons in handling a gun, you must learn to manage your dog."

" Where am I to get one?"

" I am going to give you the little liver-and-white pointer, Cap, for your very own. He is young enough to be made to know that you alone are his master, and you can make or spoil him. He may be

A FIRST LESSON IN SHOOTING

called broken now, but a wise dog keeps on learning, and you are to be his teacher."

"O, Cousin Dave, is not that a great responsibility?"

Mr. Warren smiled at the boy's earnestness. "Not too much of a responsibility. Of course I will give you a good many hints. In the first place, you alone must feed him. A large part of the road to a dog's affection lies by way of his mouth. The hand that feeds him he soon knows is the hand of a friend. Then you must take him walking with you in the fields, keeping him 'at heel' or sending him forward at your pleasure, letting him retrieve things now and then——"

"What does retrieve mean?"

"I forgot that I had not explained this to you. 'Retrieving' means bringing to you the game after you have shot it. This is a very important part of a dog's education. Many birds, when they are shot, fall in the brush and the weeds, and would be lost if the dog did not find them and carry them to his master. All my dogs are taught to bring in the birds and to hold them up to me when they reach me."

"Is this something they have to be taught?"

"Yes, but some dogs require very little teaching. It seems to be natural for them to fetch things. In England, I believe, a separate dog is used to retrieve the game, but they do not hunt in England very much as we do. The shooters generally conceal themselves behind some bank or wall, and have the birds driven over them by beaters. I have always considered this very poor sport; not much in advance of shooting tame pigeons from a trap. Czar was the most obstinate dog in refusing to retrieve that I ever tried to teach. He was very intelligent, and knew what I wanted him to do just as well as I did; but when he made up his mind not to retrieve he simply would not. He would crawl off at the word and lie down. But I kept at him, and did some pretty severe punishing, and now he enjoys retrieving as much as the other dogs. There he comes now. I will show you."

Picking up a corn-cob that lay in the field, Mr. Warren called the dog to him, and, throwing the cob as far as he could, said, "Go fetch." Away went the dog, and back he came with the cob in his

A FIRST LESSON IN SHOOTING

mouth, sitting up when he reached his master, and presenting the cob for him to take.

Rob thought, when night came, that he had had one of the most wonderful days of his life, and he went to sleep to dream of firing at clay pigeons and having the dog retrieve them.

CHAPTER IV

A SEPTEMBER WALK

IT must not be supposed that Rob spent the whole summer practising with his gun and walking about with his dog. That was not his cousin's plan for him. Mr. Warren wanted him to have a share in all the farm work that was within his strength, and in this way to discover if country life on a farm would be to his taste, acquiring at the same time all the knowledge of nature that he could. Rob entered eagerly into this plan, and in a month he could milk a cow, prune peach-trees, of which Mr. Warren had a large orchard, and do a little gardening. Later, when the haying and harvesting came on, he learned to rake hay and to help gather the sheaves of grain. But there was less of this work than there was when his father was a farm lad, because machinery nowadays does so much of it. There is no more worthless country boy than the one who thinks only of running about with his gun,

A SEPTEMBER WALK

and I want my readers to understand that **Rob** did not come within this description. But **I** am telling about his hunting experiences, not about his becoming a farmer. So we will go on with his lessons as a sportsman.

In the State where Mr. Warren lived the open season for game allowed the shooting of woodcock in July, October, November, and December; of quail, ruffed grouse, and rabbits in November and December. All the song-birds were protected at all seasons, as they should be. As has been explained, Mr. Warren did not care to hunt woodcock in the hot season. Rob did, however, get his first sight of this fine bird before the autumn arrived.

Walking out one day in early June with his cousin, two of the dogs, including Cap, of course, accompanying them, when they came to the border of a little swamp, Rob called out, "O, Cousin Dave, Cap is on a point." Surely enough he was, as stiff as if he were frozen. As Mr. Warren came up with Czar, the latter became as stiff as the other dog.

"See Czar," cried Rob, "he has a bird too."

"No, he is what we call 'backing' Cap. When

a good bird-dog sees another dog pointing, he at once, from some instinct, stops and points also. One of the most beautiful sights in the field is to see two or three dogs backing another that has a point. I have a picture of such a sight at the house that I will show you. Now let us see what Cap has found."

Thinking that it might be a nest with young birds, Mr. Warren did not let Cap go on to flush (that is, put up) the birds, but stepped in front of him himself. As he did so, a bird with a very long bill, and of a beautiful brown color, flew up. "Note that," he called to Rob; "that is a woodcock."

"What a beauty. But see. It has only flown such a short way."

"It, doubtless, has young ones here. Follow it, Rob, keeping Cap close to you, and you will probably learn something of the woodcock's intelligence."

Rob carefully approached the spot where he had seen the woodcock light, but before he got near enough for the dog to point, the bird flew up and moved away in a sort of shuffling flight, as if it was hurt.

"This woodcock has been wounded," cried Rob. "Poor thing, it cannot fly."

Woodcock — Ruffed Grouse — Quail.

"Keep on following it slowly with the dog, and see what will happen."

Rob did so, the bird continuing to get up and shuffle off every time they approached it, until it had led them some hundreds of yards from the place of discovery, when up it flew with able wing, and, turning, darted back in the direction from which it had come. Rob looked at it in blank astonishment, much to Mr. Warren's amusement.

When he rejoined his cousin, the latter parted the grass and showed him the bird's nesting-place. It was empty, but he was told that the young birds were hidden nearby, and, keeping the dogs carefully behind them, they soon discovered a downy little thing that was making itself as small as possible, and keeping perfectly still.

"That was a trick of the mother-bird," said Mr. Warren, "to draw the dog and you, too, although she feared the dog most, away from her young. Woodcock frequently do this, and so do ruffed grouse. She started back to the nest when she thought she had drawn you far enough away, but I again alarmed her, and she dropped in that clump of bushes over there. This hatching is a late one, or the birds would be larger. But such late hatches are not uncommon, and that is one reason why I object to summer woodcock shooting. These birds will not be fit to shoot in July, and yet there are too many hunters who would not hesitate to kill them if they came across them."

Mr. Warren went on to explain to Rob that the woodcock is a migratory bird, while the quail and ruffed grouse are not. The woodcock, he said, breeds perhaps in all the States, although he was not certain that it did so in the far South. Large numbers of them go far North in the early spring, and their return in October makes what are called "flights," when they are in perfect condition, and afford the finest of shooting. "Killing a fall woodcock," said he, "is quite another thing from killing a weak young bird in July. The fall birds, however, are very uncertain in their coming. We generally count on them to arrive with the full moon in October, for they are nocturnal in their habits, and both fly and feed at night. You might hunt over a piece of ground to-day, and not put up a bird, and to-morrow flush a score or more in the same place. The fall birds, too, do not confine themselves to swamps for their lighting-places. An upland, where there is a growth of brush, following the cutting off of the timber, seems to be very much to their liking, and we always look very carefully for them when we come to a clump of white birch, like that to your left. I have never ascertained whether the birds find some agreeable food under the birch to attract them, but I have a theory of my own that it is the white color of the trees, showing plainly at night, that induces them to light there."

But we were to take a walk with Rob and his cousin in September, and must be about it. It was a clear, cool day, and Mr. Warren explained to Rob that it would be a good time to look over their nearby hunting-ground, and see if there was a good prospect of birds for the later shooting. "I always want to know pretty well where the nearby birds are before going out, so as not to lose too much time hunting for them when shooting-time comes," he explained. They took Cap and Czar, and with a lunch in their pockets, were ready for a whole day's outing if need be.

Rob had already made the acquaintance of a single quail that was in the habit of singing its "bob-white" on a fence back of the house, during the nesting-season, but he was now to see the birds gathered in a flock. He had also been told the meaning of a distant drumming sound that he had heard many times repeated on the nearby mountain in the springtime. That was the drumming of the ruffed grouse, or partridge, made by striking its wings against a log. Why it did this Mr. Warren said he would not undertake to explain. He knew, however, that it was not done solely to attract a mate, because he had heard the sound as late as October. Rob had not yet seen one of these fine birds.

Their course led them across a meadow, from which a great many meadow-larks arose. Then they came to a field where wheat had been grown that year. "Here," said Mr. Warren, "we are likely to find the family of quail whose father you heard 'bob-whiting' all summer. Let us send the dogs ahead."

The dogs went willingly enough, Cap with a rush, and Czar with what perhaps he considered more dignity. They had ranged over half the field when Czar's tail began to wag with great earnestness. Mr. Warren called Rob's attention to this, telling

A SEPTEMBER WALK

him that that was what was called in sportsmen's parlance "making game"; that is, he had scented something. As Cap swung around, so that the wind blew toward him from the direction of a brushy fence, he, too, became excited, and his tail began to lash the air. "Steady, steady," Mr. Warren called to them, and the dogs moved forward, side by side. Czar drew ahead a little toward the fence, and suddenly came to a full stop, with his head turned around to the left.

"Czar has found them," cried Rob, "and see, Cap is backing him."

"Now what would you do if we were out with our guns?" asked Mr. Warren.

"Hurry up to the dogs and be ready to shoot," replied Rob.

Mr. Warren laughed one of his hearty laughs. "I knew it. A candid confession. Just what you thought you must do when you first tried to break a clay pigeon. And just what you will do in November, although you will think that you will not. Don't ever be in a hurry to shoot. I do not mean that you will not in the course of your experience, if you hunt a good many years, be required to make some quick shots, if you get those shots at all; but when you have the dogs before you telling you where the birds lie, trust them not to flush the birds, and take your time. Now, cut a good-sized cane from one of those young trees there, and then we will see what the dogs have found."

"What do you think they have?"

"Quail."

It seemed to Rob a long time before he got his cane cut, and trimmed as his cousin wanted it. Then they stepped up behind the dogs, and Mr. Warren said, "When the birds get up, count them and take good aim at one with your cane, and then tell me where they light." There was a twinkle in his eye as he said this. "Hie on," to the dogs, and with what seemed to Rob a roar, the air was apparently filled with a flock of flying quail. Cousin Dave glanced at the boy. He was staring at the flying birds, and had not even raised his stick to his shoulder. The well-trained dogs had dropped on their bellies when the birds got up.

"Make your report, Rob. First, how many were there?"

"How many? O, I could not count them. They

made such a noise when they got up, and they flew so fast, that it only seemed to me that the air was full of them. I think there must have been a hundred."

"And did you cover one or two of them with your imitation-gun?"

"I don't believe I raised my stick at all."

"But you saw where the birds went?"

"Over that ridge there, and into that thicket on the left."

"Not so bad. You forgot to shoot, and you did not count the birds, but you marked their flight very well. Let me give it as my experience in quail-shooting, that the next necessity, after the ability to hit the birds, is skill in marking them—that is, in locating the place to which they fly. I did not expect you to count them, and probably would not have done so exactly myself if we had had our guns (there were fourteen), but I wanted you to mark them. If the hunter pays no attention to the flock except to those which he has knocked down, he will make a poor bag. Quail have all sorts of notions about the cover they will seek, and to go on blindly, trusting to luck to find them again, somewhere ahead of you, means a loss of a good deal of time and many a disappointment. Therefore always try to keep your head enough to mark your birds. If you have dropped any, the dog will look out for them."

Without following up the birds they had flushed, they next directed their steps toward a piece of young woodland, this side of which was an old pasture-field, and through which ran a brook. In the middle of the field Czar "made game" and began advancing, with his nose pretty close to the ground. Cap, on the other hand, ranged off to one side, seemingly smelling in the air.

"Watch those two dogs," said Mr. Warren, "and you will have an illustration of two ways in which a dog finds game. Czar is trailing the birds. They have been out there feeding in the early morning, and Czar scents their tracks on the ground. Cap, too, gets the scent, but trailing is too slow work for him, and he is trying to locate the flock."

"Which is the better way?"

"That depends. I have known Czar to trail a flock nearly half a mile and find them, where Cap might have missed them entirely. On the other

A SEPTEMBER WALK

hand, Cap's quickness will often bring him within pointing distance of birds before Czar has arrived there. In the South, where the fields are large, and there are a good many birds, a slow dog will not do at all."

Czar had now reached the edge of the woods, and was showing by his actions that the trail was getting very warm, when there was a rush of wings, and up got the birds quite out of gunshot.

"Was that Czar's fault?" asked Rob.

"No; the birds were running to the brook, and they simply did not lie for him to point. This often happens with running birds."

In the course of the forenoon they found six flocks of quail, and Rob so far mastered his nervousness that he counted the last two flocks, and took such good aim at some of the birds (by his own reckoning) that he thought they would certainly have fallen had his stick been a gun.

About noon they stopped at a fine spring and ate their lunch, and then Mr. Warren announced his intention to turn toward the mountain, in the hope of showing Rob a grouse. Grouse, he explained, when they trudged on, are hatched in flocks, just as quail are, the female laying from nine to fifteen eggs. In the early autumn the whole flock is sometimes flushed at once; but the birds soon separate, and later it is usual to find two together rather than a larger number. They are great travellers, and it is never certain where they will be found, no matter how well they have been marked in the late summer. This makes it necessary for the grouse-hunter to be a good walker. They like wooded regions, and if there is a swamp in the midst of a wood, they may be found near it, and will certainly plunge into it when flushed. One thing favors the grouse-hunter. The birds are pretty straight flyers, and if the course of one is taken, there is a fair chance of flushing it again. But the chase may be a long and tiresome one.

"Are they hard to shoot?" asked Rob.

"Yes and no. Yes, because they are so often found in the thick cover, and because they do not lie well to a dog. Cap would not be worth a cent for partridges, because he would not hunt them slowly enough. Many partridge-hunters say the only use they have for a dog is to find dead birds, but I do not agree with them. If Czar crosses a

A SEPTEMBER WALK

partridge's track, he will begin to trail, and if he comes to a fallen tree, he knows just as well as I do that the bird is likely to be there, and will almost crawl within pointing distance. As to the other side of my answer, I should say that the partridge is not a hard bird to shoot if you get it in fairly open ground, because it is a large mark, and it flies straight. It does fly very swiftly and possesses great vitality, and many a hard-hit bird gets away. In one respect the ruffed grouse is very stupid. In the big woods, like the Adirondacks, it is easily treed by the barking of a dog, and a whole flock will sometimes sit in the branches and let themselves be picked off one by one by a gunner, so long as the dog keeps up his barking, and only the lower birds are shot first. If a bird is shot from the higher branches, it seems to frighten those below as it falls past them. My theory is that the birds there take the dog for their traditional enemy the fox, and think they are safe so long as they are in a tree. I flushed a flock in Maine once with a red Irish setter that did resemble a fox, and one of the birds, sitting on the limb of a young sapling, allowed me to walk under it and hit it with the end of my gun-barrel, before it flew, all the time craning its neck to keep the dog in sight."

"O, Cousin Dave," said Rob, "how much you do know about birds."

When they got part way up the mountain-side, a sound like a distant rumble of thunder reached their ears. That, Rob was told, was a partridge that had been frightened by their footsteps. Rob thought it must be a pretty big bird that could make so much noise in its flight. Another and another of the birds made itself heard but not seen as they proceeded, although they kept both dogs at heel. Presently they came to an old wagon-track—hardly a road—through the woods, and as they stepped into this, Mr. Warren pulled Rob back suddenly, by a grasp on his shoulder. "Do you see that partridge in the roadway yonder?" he asked, himself excited now. Rob looked, but could see nothing. "Right in the path, beyond that yellow leaf." No, Rob could see no bird.

"This is an excellent example of the protection that nature gives the partridge in its coloring. It is only by chance that my eye caught it. 'Charge, charge,' (to each dog). The bird sees us perfectly,

A SEPTEMBER WALK

and is watching us, but it is foolish enough to think that we do not see it. Now I am going to make you see it. Do precisely as I tell you. You see this wagon-track starting by my foot. Follow it with your eye until you come opposite the chestnut-tree (Rob could distinguish a good many trees by their leaves or bark by this time), on which some woodman has cut a mark. Good. Beyond that you see a rotten stump, just out of the road. Yes. Now look in the roadway, half-way from that stump to the yellow leaf opposite it. What do you see?"

"Only brown leaves."

"Those brown leaves are the partridge. There, now, did you not see it turn its neck?"

"I did, I did," cried Rob. "I distinguish it plainly now. How wonderfully it matches the ground and leaves."

"Take a good look at it, and then approach it with Czar. You may get a point."

But he did not. As soon as the boy stepped fairly into the road the bird rose, with a tremendous whirring, and was out of sight.

"That was grand," said Rob. "I would have walked all day for that sight."

"You were lucky to get a sight of a partridge sitting. It does not occur too often in the same circumstances. But you may see one quite often later in the season, if you watch in the old orchard about sundown. They come down there then to 'bud,' that is, to eat the buds when the snow covers up their own berries."

It seemed to Rob, as he walked home, that, to be able to kill a partridge on the wing would be to satisfy his highest ambition.

CHAPTER V

ROB'S FIRST DAY'S HUNT

NO boy ever went to bed with more eager anticipation of Christmas morning than did Rob, on the night of October 31st, with his first day's hunt to come with the opening of the season on the morrow. His cousin had seen that he was properly equipped. He had a hunting-suit, made of light-brown canvas, which would stand the briars, and which was fitted with big game-pockets. With this went a pair of heavy shoes, the soles studded with hob-nails, to prevent his feet from slipping on the rocks and leaves. His hat was a soft, felt one, and to protect his hands from the briars he was to wear a pair of old walking-gloves, the fingers of which had been cut short.

Rob was dressed before daybreak, but his cousin took his time in setting out, saying that he always liked to give the quail time to begin feeding before getting on the ground, as, in this way, there was a better opportunity for the dogs to scent them.

The morning was an ideal one. The air was pretty cold, there was no wind, and the sky was overcast with a thin haze. Preceding frosts had cut down the more tender weeds and shrivelled the leaves of the taller ones on their stalks, and the rime of the night just past lay thick on pasture and stubble. In the woods most of the trees, except some of the oaks, had dropped their leaves, giving the hunters a good view of any birds that might fly up before them.

Their first hunting-ground was in the field where they had put up the flock in September, and the dogs were "hied on" when the wheat stubble was reached. This the dogs ranged without "making game." But as soon as Cap had leaped the fence he came to a point.

"I think these birds are lazy," said Mr. Warren. "They do not seem to have travelled much yet, and it was good luck that Cap did not land right in the midst of them."

"Are you sure they're there?" asked Rob.

"Not absolutely sure, since Cap may scent a rabbit, but I think it is the quail. Now let us plan a little. Here to the left is a thick growth of young trees which would make bad cover for us. We will, therefore, step around on that side and flush the birds ourselves, and they will probably fly toward that weedy field, where we ought to have good sport with them. Are you excited?"

"I suppose I am," Rob confessed.

"Naturally, of course. Now try to remember one thing. You will kill only the bird you aim at; so don't make the mistake of shooting at the flock. I remember well the proof I had of the value of this advice in my younger days. I was hunting in Maryland, and late one afternoon four of our party met at the edge of a big swale, and as we came up, one of the dogs pointed and the other three backed him. My companion, who knew the ground well, said, 'Boys, we shall get only the birds out of this flock that we kill when they fly up, as the swale in front of us is practically impenetrable.' So each man made up his mind to kill two birds as they rose. We put up the birds, and a bigger flock I never saw flushed. There were, I remember, two big oak-trees in front of us, about one hundred feet apart, and when those birds rose it seemed to me that the space between these trees was simply full of birds. Well, each of us fired his two barrels, and, crouching to look under the smoke (we were using black powder), I could not see a bird fall. 'How many did we get?' asked my companion. 'Not a bird,' said the man on the right, who had the best view. And not a bird it was. Then each of us confessed that the air seemed so full of birds that he had simply fired at the flock. I have never understood yet how every bird escaped that rain of shot, but I have never forgotten the lesson."

Mr. Warren had gone into these details of his story with a purpose, desiring to allow Rob to rid himself of the first nervousness caused by the discovery of the game. "Now," said he, "we will put up the birds. Be sure to mark their flight."

At the word "Go on, Cap," the dog moved forward, and a fine flock of quail rose. "Bang, bang," went Rob's gun. "Too quick," said his cousin, who, taking his time, fired at two of the hind birds, both of which fell.

"Didn't I kill any?" asked Rob.

"Not a feather. You shot too quick, and you did not aim. I know just how you felt. You thought the birds were getting away from you, and yet I had time to kill two after you had fired both barrels. But you need not mind that. Some really good shots get rattled when a flock rises, and fill their bags from the scattered birds. You saw where they went?"

"Yes, I remembered that advice. Most of them went straight ahead."

The dogs were sent forward to retrieve the two dead birds, and then they went on after the rest. On the way Mr. Warren explained that it was not well to follow up a scattered flock too rapidly. Some persons, he said, had a theory that birds could "withhold their scent." He did not believe this, but thought that when a dog did not scent a recently flushed bird it was because that bird had simply dropped down and remained stationary, with folded wings, thus not actually "withholding" its scent, but not giving out any. The field toward which the birds had flown was good cover, with a rank growth of ragweed, and when Tass, the other dog they had with them, reached the centre of the field, she pointed, and Cap did the same to her right.

"There are two of the birds," said Mr. Warren. "You go over and shoot the one in front of your dog, and I will try for the one that Tass is pointing. Take it easy. You can depend on your dog."

Rob kept telling himself, as he went along, that he would "keep perfectly cool," and he stopped a moment before giving Cap the order to flush the bird. When he did so, and the bird rose, he "kept his head," and, as the bird flew directly from him, he did cover it, and at the sound of the gun down went the quail.

"Good enough," shouted his cousin; "now step back a little till I shoot."

Mr. Warren brought down his bird, and the dogs, after retrieving, were sent forward to find the rest. Rob's good shot had given him confidence, and he killed one more of three birds at which he shot, a very good average, he was assured, for a boy with his experience. When they had killed eight of these birds Mr. Warren proposed to leave the rest, as he did not believe in killing off a whole flock, as perhaps, in such open cover, they might have done.

Their course next brought them to an upland "cut-off"—a new growth where the trees had been cut in recent years—and that, Mr. Warren remarked, was a likely place for fall woodcock. The October full moon had come early that year, and the weather had been warm, and for these reasons the October flight of woodcock had been a disappointment, and Mr. Warren thought it not at all unlikely that they would find some of the birds that day. As soon as they entered the "cut-off," Tass made game, and pointed very quickly.

"Probably a woodcock," said Mr. Warren. "The brush here is a little thick, and I think I will try for this bird while you observe me. Take note of its manner of flight. There will be no whir, as with a quail, but the bird will spring upward, and then direct its flight as it may see fit. Woodcock do not make a long flight, but in bad cover it is often puzzling to locate them, as they twist and turn, and then literally flop down where they please."

The bird, when flushed, was indeed a woodcock, and Mr. Warren dropped it easily, after letting it get far enough away to escape being torn by the shot. When told to "go fetch," Tass started forward, but before coming to the dead bird she pointed again.

"Another cock, upon my word," exclaimed Mr. Warren. "I do believe there has been a flight during the night. It is fairly open there. Try your luck, Rob. Don't shoot until the bird has started off horizontally."

Rob walked up to the dog, and the bird, which was lying almost under her nose, took flight. Bang went Rob's gun, the warning against haste being forgotten, and on went the bird. But it did not go far. Cousin Dave's gun sounded, and it dropped within easy gunshot.

"Now, Rob, you have let me do what in shooters' parlance is called 'wipe your nose.' That means kill the bird after you had missed it. I saw it was too fine a bird to lose, and you left me plenty of time to shoot after you."

"I knew I shot too quickly as soon as my gun went off, but in this brush I felt as if the bird would get away."

"Practice and experience will overcome that. Look at Cap, he has been pointing behind that

ROB'S FIRST DAY'S HUNT

clump while we have been talking. It is open there; try again."

This time Rob took pains, firing as the bird (another woodcock) turned, and he dropped it nicely.

"Only to think," he exclaimed, "I have killed two quail and a woodcock before ten o'clock. I do wish father could be with us."

"So do I, and I am not sure that he would do as well as his son."

They got five woodcock in all in that "cut-off," and Rob had to stop and lay them all on the grass and admire their beautiful color, and wonder at the length of their bills. When his cousin told him that some of the snipe family, to which this bird belongs, have bills twice as long, Rob thought these bills must be very much in the birds' way.

Near the other side of the "cut-off" was a pile of brush, which Mr. Warren said looked like a good place for a rabbit's resting-place, and he suggested that Rob give it a kick. With his gun ready, Rob did so, and out went a rabbit at the first jar. "Easy, easy," called Mr. Warren; "he is going slow. Aim at his head." Rob was careful with his aim, and he knocked the rabbit over very neatly, receiving praise from his cousin for the shot. Cap was just as willing to retrieve the rabbit as to fetch a bird, and when Rob had it in hand his cousin laughingly said, "Now do you know what you are in for?" "What?" asked Rob. "Lugging that weight all the rest of the day." Rob declared that he did not mind this in the least, but he found the rabbit rather awkward to get into his game-pocket, and, before the day was over, he agreed that it would be a good plan to kill one's rabbits on the way home.

The next field they hunted proved to be a disappointment, no birds being found; but half a mile farther the dogs pointed. When the birds—they were quail—rose, Mr. Warren killed with his right barrel and missed with his left, and Rob succeeded in firing only once, and that without effect. The birds disappeared over a ridge, and they had only their general direction to assist in finding them again. And they did not find them. As is not infrequently the case with quail, they had turned in their flight, and lit just where their pursuers did not look. The hunters sat down on a fence, and Mr. Warren tried the experiment of calling the birds, but this, too, was a failure. It gave him an opportunity, however, to explain to Rob that the quail changes its call in the autumn, and instead of whistling "bob white" gives out a note which the farmers' boys sometimes translate into "bu-u-ckwheat." When a flock that has been scattered cannot be found by the dogs, the hunter sometimes, by whistling this call, can get a reply, and thus find out what direction the birds have taken. But these birds had either flown out of reach of the call or refused to be deceived by it. So finally they were given up.

"It is nearly noon," said Mr. Warren, "and I am hungry. Let us go to the head of the gully you see over there, where there is a fine spring, and eat our lunch."

This was entirely to Rob's inclination, but the lunch was delayed a little. The gully before them was fringed with a young growth of trees, including some white birches, and when the dogs were sent into this growth both at once pointed. Rob was sent ahead to get the shot, and he flushed another woodcock. The bird flew directly over his head, and turned to seek cover in the gully, and as it did so

Mr. Warren cried, "Now is your chance," and Rob fired and down came the bird. He was again warmly praised for the shot.

Then they witnessed a wonderful piece of dogwork. Tass had seen the bird fall, and she was given the command to fetch it. With the bird in her mouth she was coming back, when suddenly her neck bent to one side, and she pointed as stiffly as could be.

"Look at that, Rob. I never saw that done but once before. Tass is pointing a live bird with a dead one in her mouth."

"Would you think it possible for her to distinguish the second bird with the other one under her nose?"

"No, it is very wonderful. My theory is that she distinguishes the fresh scent in some way from the scent of the dead bird. But that is all conjecture. How many things dogs could tell us if only they could talk."

The second bird came out near Mr. Warren and fell when he fired.

Before they got to the spring Tass pointed again, and on Mr. Warren stepping up to her, two woodcock flew up at once, one going straight ahead and one to the right. As both barrels of Mr. Warren's gun sounded, the two birds dropped.

"O, Cousin Dave," said Rob. "What a wonderful shot you are. I never shall be able to do that."

"Not a wonderful shot for a man of my experience, Rob, and at woodcock. When you have killed a partridge with each barrel, both rising at once, and each going in the opposite direction, you may do a little boasting."

No more birds interrupted their walk to the spring, and they found a mossy seat and took out their parcels of sandwiches, and enjoyed their luncheon. "Take plenty of time," said Cousin Dave, who was constitutionally opposed to depriving himself of any of the pleasure of a meal. "Hunters who hurry at lunch are sure to get tired out, and a tired-out man can never shoot well." When their repast was finished, while Cousin Dave enjoyed his pipe, Rob had to take his game out of his pockets and again admire the plumpness and plumage of the birds and the size of the rabbit. He declared that the latter had not yet increased in weight, and that he was willing to carry two or three more if he could shoot them.

When they were ready to start, Mr. Warren asked Rob if he would prefer to look for more quail, or to walk a mile to the mountain and ascend it, with the hope of getting some shots at partridges. "We have," said he, "now in our pockets nine quail and nine woodcock—a very good morning's work. So, if you like, we can take our chances with the partridges; but I tell you in advance that the result is very uncertain."

Rob thought it would be a grand achievement to round out their day with a couple of the bigger birds, and so off they started for the higher wooded ground. As they walked along, Rob asked if his cousin often got so great a variety of game in one day. He was told that this could not be counted on, as, later in the season, they would find no woodcock, and might not hunt where the partridges kept. "I had a peculiar experience in the way of variety a number of years ago, when I was hunting in another part of this State. We were approaching a sharp precipice of sheer rock, that rose some two hundred feet in height. A few hundred yards from its top

I kicked out a rabbit, and before I had shot, the rabbit ran plump into a small flock of quail. I killed one of these, and then got the rabbit, which could not go far because of the precipice in front, and came back to give me an easy shot. I lined the quail, and we (there were two of us) climbed down the face of the rock as best we could to pursue them. Just as I reached the bottom, my dog pointed and so did my friend's. When we started the dogs on, a woodcock got up in front of mine and a partridge in front of the other. I killed the cock, and, as the other bird tried to get right up to the top of the rock, it made a beautiful target for the other gun. I can see it yet as it spread its wings and tail, when hit, and settled gracefully to the ground. Here, then, we had killed a quail, a rabbit, a woodcock, and a partridge, all within the space of twenty minutes, and all within less than a quarter of a mile of one another."

When they got pretty well up the mountain-side, Cap was called to heel, and Tass was constantly admonished by her master to go slowly. There were still leaves on some of the trees, especially the oaks, and the leaves on the ground were dry, making the walking noisy, all of which was in favor of the birds and against the hunters. Coming to a growth of laurels, Tass made game, and Cap was allowed to go forward a little. He at once threw his nose into the air, and wheeling to the left, pointed toward a laurel-bush. "I believe your dog has found the first bird," said his cousin to Rob. "Will you try for it?"

"What do you advise?" asked Rob.

"We will both walk up toward it. If it lies and gives a good shot, I will wait for you to shoot first, but if it does not, I will see what I can do. We want one partridge at least to make up our variety."

The bird did not lie well, rising with a roar, as it seemed to Rob, as soon as they advanced, and disappearing behind the bushes just as Mr. Warren's gun sounded. "I guess you missed him, Cousin Dave," said Rob. "He went right on."

"Did you see him after he turned the bushes?"

"No."

"Then he may be our bird yet. It was almost a snap-shot, but I had the gun well on him. Tass, fetch dead."

The dog rushed through the laurel growth, and

disappeared in the brush beyond. In a few moments they heard her footsteps on the leaves, and when they got sight of her she had the bird in her mouth, looking as proud as if she herself had shot it.

"What a wonderful dog," cried Rob. "Did she see the bird fall?"

"No, but she saw the direction in which it went, and followed that direction until she found it lying dead. If you will heft the bird you will see how heavy it is, and will understand how easily a partridge, even when hard hit, can fly a long distance."

Rob admired the fine bird, smoothing its feathers, and saying that to kill such a one would be the height of his ambition.

Calling Cap to heel again, they continued their walk, Mr. Warren giving Rob some instruction about partridge-shooting as they walked. "You will read in books and in sporting papers a good deal about the necessity of aiming well ahead of a partridge if it flies crosswise from you. Of course the bird is going very fast, and it requires an appreciable time for the shot to get where the bird is after the firing of the gun. But it is my experience that I am never conscious of aiming *ahead* of the bird. It is a matter of practice to know when to fire and where to aim, and, as the gun is being swung along in the same direction that the bird is flying, the muzzle is naturally carried somewhat in advance. You must simply 'cover' the bird, and this means only that you must aim where the shot will tell. I do that intuitively. Doubtless, I should kill sometimes when I miss if the gun was pointed farther in advance; but you know that we miss clay birds from the trap, where no such nice calculation is needed, and this shows that the most careful aim is sometimes unsuccessful. You have to take a good many snap-shots at partridges, that is, shots fired without deliberate aim. There is not time to aim carefully before the bird will disappear behind some cover, and you fire, trusting to luck to kill. Some men seem to be natural snap-shots, and it is surprising how often they will make such shots tell. Hark! there went up a partridge, and there goes another."

They had now reached the top of a ridge, beyond which was a more open growth, and Rob was told to have his gun in readiness, as a bird was likely to get up at any moment. Tass was moving on to the left of them when a partridge rose almost at Rob's feet. "Take your time," called his cousin, and Rob fired, to see quite a puff of feathers leave the bird. "Good shot, if you didn't down him," said Mr. Warren. "That was the time when you aimed a little too far behind."

"Do you think the dog would be able to find it?"

"No, it was not hit in the body. But we may put it up again. Sometimes a bird thus hit will lie harder."

Following up the direction of this bird, Tass pointed toward a fallen tree-top. "That's probably your bird, Rob. Walk up to the right of the tree-top." But Rob was not fortunate. The bird went out the other side, and fell before Mr. Warren's gun. "Sorry, Rob," said he, "but such is the fortune of bird-war."

They now turned their steps toward home, as it was getting late, and Rob got no other shot at partridges that day. But he did kill one more quail, and Mr. Warren got three, so that they went home with thirteen quail, nine woodcock, and two partridges. His cousin told him that they could by no means always count on making so good a bag, no matter how well they shot, and assured him that he had done himself credit in the part he had taken in securing the game.

Rob declared to his Cousin Annie that he was not *very* tired, but he was sound asleep a few minutes after supper, curled up on the lounge, and he did confess the next day that his legs were a *little sore.*

CHAPTER VI

SHOOTING BAY-SNIPE

ROB made a long visit at home that winter, and while there his future plans were carefully discussed by his parents. He himself declared that he liked country life, and expressed a wish to spend at least another year at the farm. It was finally decided that he should do so, as he was growing strong and ruddy, and was young enough to take up a business pursuit later, if he should not make the country his permanent home. His cousin had a good library, and he began a course of reading during the winter, and carried on some of his studies with his cousin's help. For Cousin Dave was as good a mathematician as he was a shot, and more than one puzzle in algebra that Rob could not solve was unravelled with his cousin's aid.

Mr. Warren had a good many books on the subject of hunting, and Rob found them intensely interesting. One evening in the following spring, as he was reading one of them, he asked, "Cousin Dave, what are bay-snipe?"

"Members of the family *scolopacidae*."

"That might satisfy a young Roman, but just what are they to a young American?"

"Well, in United States language, they are a large membership of the snipe family, which breed in the North and begin their migration in the early summer, continuing it until late in the autumn. Your geography will show you that a large part of our Atlantic coast is separated from the ocean by a series of bays divided in turn from the ocean by narrow strips of sandy beach. These bays and adjacent islands are favorite feeding-places for such snipe, and in the East the birds have obtained the name 'bay-snipe.' But they are an inland bird, too, and perhaps as many lay their course south by way of the Western plains to the Gulf of Mexico, and so still farther South, as by way of our coast. And, by the by, I have been thinking of taking you to the coast for a snipe-shoot this summer, if you would like to go."

Rob was, of course, delighted, and began to read

with interest a book on this kind of shooting, which his cousin pointed out to him.

So it happened that one evening, early in August, the two sportsmen found themselves at the depot of a little village near the east end of Shinnecock Bay, on the south shore of Long Island, where a rather dilapidated horse and wagon met them, and conveyed them to the house of the bayman who was to attend them in their shooting. Rob found John, the bayman, a very interesting character, and learned on better acquaintance that he was a synonym of good-nature, and an expert in the ways of bay-snipe.

"What time do we start out in the morning?" Rob asked, after they had had their supper, and he had been listening to a discussion of the chances of sport between John and his cousin.

"Well," drawled John, "the wind's bin east fur four days, and I cal'late it will blow south to-morrow, and if it does, there ought to be birds. So we'll be about pretty spry. It is sun-up at five, so I guess mother will have breakfast at half-past three, and we'll be gettin' across the bay half an hour later. There's a lot o' folks after snipe, and I don't propose to let them get all the good places."

Rob had many questions to ask, and he learned from John's answers that the snipe generally flew against the wind, and that a flight was, therefore, looked for when the wind blew up the coast from the south or southwest. John explained that a good shooting-place was a little projection on the bay side of the beach, with shoal water in front, in which to place their "stools" (decoy birds made of wood), where they would be most likely to attract the eye of the live birds.

It seemed to Rob that he had just fallen asleep when he was aroused by John's cheery cry of "Breakfast," but he was soon dressed and doing his part in disposing of a goodly supply of ham and eggs and corn-bread. Then they made their way to a little creek nearby, in which lay John's sail-boat, and were soon being poled to the bay by John, as the wind was light and contrary, and the creek narrow. Once on the broader water John hoisted the sail, and with more wind they made fair progress across the bay.

Rob found the sail a very interesting one, as he was new to bay scenery. In the dim light he could just distinguish the low-lying beach on the ocean side, and the higher ground of the mainland, and

SHOOTING BAY-SNIPE

before them twinkled the bright eye of the lighthouse that stands on a projection of the Long Island coast. Presently he heard in the air above a repeated " quawk, quawk," made by some bird on the move. " Is that a snipe ? " he asked. " No," replied John, " that's a quawk." His cousin further explained that this is a name given to the bird sometimes on account of its cry, but that its real name is night heron, and that it is over two feet long, and the female has long white plumes growing from the top of the head. It is not a table-bird, and is more frequently heard than seen, since it feeds at night on the marshes, retiring to wooded swamps by day.

As it grew lighter they saw that only one boat was ahead of them going in their direction, and John said he would have no trouble to secure the shooting-ground he had in view, and in another half-hour they arrived there.

Sailing as close to the shore as they could, John threw overboard a light anchor and said, " Now, gentlemen, we must do some wading." All wore rubber-boots, and Rob and his cousin waded ashore, while John put out the stools. Rob watched this business with much interest. There were between forty and fifty of the stools, representing different varieties of the snipe, and all of wood, although his cousin told him that tin ones were a good deal used. Into the bottom of each of these stools John inserted a stick about two feet long, and these sticks were then thrust into the mud, about thirty yards from the edge of the shore where they were to shoot, and so disposed as to resemble as closely as possible a flock of real snipe. This done to his satisfaction, John poled the sail-boat away for a distance of a quarter of a mile, in order that it might not frighten the birds, and came back in a small row-boat which he easily disposed of in the grass.

While he was gone, Mr. Warren and Rob had been cutting a bunch of branches from a growth of bushes nearby, with which to make their "blind." These branches were stuck into the soft ground, opposite the stools, arranged so as to resemble a natural clump of bushes, and to conceal the men behind them when they sat. Inside the blind two rubber blankets were laid down, and each shooter then took his seat, with his gun at hand and a box containing his cartridges by his side. Cousin Dave lighted his pipe and, stretching himself out, declared that he was perfectly happy, whether the birds came or not. "Snipe-shooting is a lazy man's sport," said he, "and it grows on a man as he gets older. The famous Gov. Dix had a country place not many miles from here, and he spent many hours of his later days in his snipe-blind."

"Yes," said John, "he had a wooden seat in his blind, with a back, and they do say he killed a power of snipe."

It was daylight now, and Rob was just going to ask when the first snipe would probably come along, when John sat up and began to whistle. He did not whistle a tune, but something that went like "f-e-w, few, few," repeated many times. Rob had read that the hunter whistled to the snipe, but he had no idea just how this was done. Mr. Warren explained that John's trained and acute ear had distinguished the whistle of a snipe up the bay, and he was trying to attract it. Now Rob distinctly heard the answering call, and soon his cousin directed his attention to a flock of more than a dozen birds that were making their way down the bay.

John kept "talking" to them, varying his note

with his acquired skill to represent different notes of the real birds, and the latter soon turned their course, and came directly for the stools.

"Now, Rob, we are going to get a shot, and you must remember the first axiom of bay-shooting, whether it is at snipes or ducks, and that is that the distance over water is mighty deceptive. Don't fire till I say 'shoot,' and then aim right at the birds' beaks. They will swing up against the wind."

Rob peered with excited interest at the approaching birds through a little opening in the blind, and it did seem to him that they were near enough long before his cousin gave the word, and when this was given he saw only a confused collection of legs and wings. "Take the forward birds. Fire," said Mr. Warren. Rob got two birds with his first barrel, but missed with his second, and Mr. Warren got one with each.

John, who was not supposed to do much shooting, cried "down" to Rob, who started to rise to his feet, and kept on whistling, and the remaining birds, after flying off a short distance, turned again to the stools and gave them another shot. This time Rob killed one with each barrel, and Mr. Warren got his

Bay-Snipe Shooting.

shot into a bunch of four, killing all of them and dropping another with his second barrel. The rest flew away.

"Pretty good shootin'," said John. "The boy handles his gun right well."

"Of course. I taught him," laughed Cousin Dave.

"O, that accounts for it, does it?" replied John. "I thought it was the gentle way I called 'em in."

Rob was allowed to wade out and gather up the birds. As he did not identify them from the pictures he had seen, he was told that they were little yellow legs (called also lesser tell-tales in the books). They were about as big as a robin, with ashy-brown feathers and a bill of two inches. He thought they did not compare with the upland birds which he had shot the autumn before, but he was greatly interested in the manner of calling them and watching them come in. To his remark about their size John replied, "O, there's bigger snipe than little yeller legs. There's a big yeller leg that looks jest like these, only it is bigger, and there's willets and red marlins, and other good-sized birds. And when it comes to fine eatin' birds, your woodcock ain't no ways ahead of a black-breast plover. I swunnie, I hear a big yeller leg now," and he began to whistle.

The sound came faintly from far above them, but finally Rob, following its direction, could see a speck in the dull sky which John said was the bird. It was ready for company, and pretty soon it began to lower itself, and came up toward the stools, with easy wing. "It's your bird," Mr. Warren said to Rob, and the latter dropped it right among the stools.

"All right that time," said John. "But, young man, I want you to be mighty keerful and not shoot into my stools. They take time to make and time to paint, and I allow there ain't a nicer lot on the bay."

Rob promised to be very careful, and he again waded out and retrieved the bird. It was nearly as large again as the other ones, and he thought it quite worth a sportsman's attention.

As soon as they were settled down again John began to whistle once more, and Rob's attention was directed to a bunch of birds that were making their way toward them close to the shore. "Dowitchers,"

SHOOTING BAY-SNIPE

John explained, between whistles. There were ten of them, and they came in directly over the stools, and swung round ready to light, if the water had been shallow enough. All three fired at these birds, and, as they were well bunched, all fell but two, and these came back and were shot, one by Rob and one by Mr. Warren. When Rob had picked them up he found them about the size of the smaller birds they had first shot, but with a ruddier breast. He was told that they often came in very large flocks, and that they were sold in the city markets as "English," or properly speaking, Wilson's snipe.

"I must say," remarked Rob, "that I have not a very high opinion of snipe intelligence. I did not think any bird would refuse to fly away when it had such warning as we have given these with our guns."

"A snipe is a fool bird for sure," said John. "They can be took in easier than a countryman in New York City. Why, one spring I was over on the beach, without any decoys, one day, when I see there was a stir of snipe. You know they fly north in the spring. So what does I do but make a lot of mud balls and stick them on some sticks in the water, and I give you the truth them birds stooled to them mud balls just as easy as you please, and I killed thirty-five and then my powder give out."

"I grant that these snipe are not over-intelligent," remarked Cousin Dave, "and certainly they are not timid. But you must remember that we are taking the biggest kind of an advantage of them. Here we are hidden, looking just like the rest of the shore, and in front of us are a very natural-looking flock of snipe. Suppose you were in a flock of your fellow-birds, looking for a place to feed, and you saw some forty of your kind apparently enjoying a good meal. You, too, would stop, especially if you, by whistle, were hospitably invited to. And if you were startled by a sound like thunder as you drew near, but you saw half a dozen of your fellows apparently lighting, after the thunder ceased, you would, doubtless, wheel round as these birds did, and try again to light. When you match a man against a bird, the man, if he knows his business, will win."

So Mr. Warren and John smoked, and they all talked, and not a half-hour passed without a shot at something, for the birds were on the move. After

SHOOTING BAY-SNIPE

ten o'clock fewer were seen, but John predicted more sport in the afternoon.

Their collection now embraced, besides the varieties mentioned, two of the black-breasted plover which John had so lauded, and which were so fat that one of them, shot when flying quite high by Rob, burst its breast open when it struck the ground. They had a few robin snipe (red-breasted sandpipers); one turnstone, or calico-black, as John called it, with plumage pied in white, black, brown, and chestnut; and two upland plover, a bird highly prized by epicures, and both shot as a flock passed over at a good height, by Mr. Warren. John declared that there was an old sportsman staying at one of the shore houses who would have given five dollars to have killed those plover, as it was his boast that he had killed the first of them taken on Shinnecock Bay every year since 1860.

An amusing incident occurred at noon, as they were eating their lunch. Rob had noticed that John carried a lunch-pail of his own, although the basket provided for him and his cousin seemed to him ample for the three. When John uncovered this, Rob remarked on the generous supply, and John replied that if there was any one thing he did like to do, it was to eat, and that he had found that, if he did not look out for himself, no one would look out for him. As they sat in the blind, disposing of sandwiches, cold-boiled eggs, etc., the whistle of a snipe struck John's ear. Just at that moment he had bitten off about one-half of a large triangular piece of pie. When he heard the sound, he made frantic efforts to dispose of the pie, and, not succeeding quickly enough, he then tried to whistle with his mouth full. This being also an impossibility, he cried: "For mercy's sake, whistle; whistle something, if it's only Yankee Doodle." Mr. Warren was no mean snipe-whistler, but he was so overcome with laughter at John's efforts that he could at first make no sound. Rob did his best to imitate the call, and with Mr. Warren's assistance noise enough was made to attract the attention of the birds—a small flock of little yellow legs—and they got four of them. When Rob came back to the blind with the birds, he found John on his back, laughing till the tears came. "What is the matter?" he inquired. "O," said John, "the noise you two made when you got at it! I guess those birds must have thought there was a snipe camp-meetin' going on here."

There were two incidents in the way of variety in the afternoon. Looking off to the west John remarked, "I do believe there is a flock of willet." Mr. Warren thought so, too, but they were not certain that they would get a shot at them, as the birds in their flight would pass near another point on which there were shooters. "I know one thing," said John, "ef the man with Pete Lane can't whistle willet no better than Pete, no willet won't take no notice of them. He seems to whistle yeller leg to everything."

How badly Pete whistled they did not actually know, as they were too distant to hear, but at any rate the birds kept on, and, liking John's music, made a direct line for their stools.

"There's six of them birds," said John, "and I propose we let Robbie kill 'em all, and give him no supper if he don't." Mr. Warren agreed to this, and Rob said he would stake his supper. John assured him that the willet was the biggest fool of all the snipe family, and that, if he got one wounded bird down, it would squawk and all the others would come back as often as required.

When the birds came near, Rob found them so large that his nerve began to become a little agitated, but his cousin said, quietly, "No hurry, now," and he braced up. They let him take his own time to shoot, and he brought down a bird with each barrel. One of these was only wounded, and it made good John's prediction about its squalling capacity, and back came the other birds. Rob was ready for them and got two with the right barrel and one with the left, and then he declared that he would let the other go, although it came back again and again until he went out to pick up the dead ones.

He found the birds larger than any he had shot, with partly webbed toes, and their plumage gray, with black marks, and white underneath. John gave him the opinion that they were as poor a table-bird as were shot on the bay, but Mr. Warren told John that he had no opinion of the judgment of an epicure who confessed to liking bitterns.

They had good sport later in the afternoon, and among the birds that came to them were two large ones, one of which Rob killed, that John called red marlin, the book-name being great marbled godwit. These birds were colored like a woodcock, stood on legs five inches long, and had bills as long as their legs. John said he had seen some large flocks of them, but had never killed many, and did not "just remember how they et." "All bay-snipe taste alike to me," said Cousin Dave, "and I think a little onion in the pot improves the best of them."

Rob and his cousin spent five days on the bay, not getting so good sport every day, but never going in without some birds. Rob found the practice very much to his benefit. He had no nervous inclination to overcome, as when a dog was pointing a bird before him in cover; and he was able to take aim at the slow-flying snipe, and thus to calculate his shots.

On the last afternoon they were out they had the good fortune to add to their variety two sickle-bill curlews. The birds came flying along well out in the bay, when John spied them, but he recognized them at once and warned Rob that they were a prize, and they looked as big as chickens to the boy when they came in. Rob was allowed to kill both of them, and was very proud over his achievement. Their total length was some two feet, and their curved bills were about eight inches long. John said that in his grandfather's day he had been told that they often appeared in large numbers, but in later years they had become somewhat scarce.

In contrast with these big birds were frequent flocks of the tiny snipe known on that bay as the ox-eye. Often fifty of them would come scurrying by, and John would call them in with a flat, tin mouth-whistle. He said that the market gunners shot them when they could kill a dozen or more with one barrel, as they brought about seventy-five cents a dozen in New York, but Mr. Warren, who was utterly opposed to taking life unnecessarily, refused to shoot at them, saying that they had all the larger birds that they wanted for the table, and, of course, he never shot game to sell.

Before the week was over, Rob found that, while bay-snipe shooting was lazy sport, so far as exercise was concerned, it subjected him to a sunburning that turned his face into a bright red, and caused the skin to peel from his nose. A broad-brimmed hat did not suffice to shield him from the reflected rays of the sun, and both he and his cousin carried home faces that belied their strict temperance principles.

SHOOTING BAY-SNIPE

It was so warm that they did not try to take any of the birds home with them to eat, but Rob took several to the city to be set up by a taxidermist, as the beginning of a collection which he had decided to make.

CHAPTER VII

A TRIP TO THE ADIRONDACKS

AMONG Mr. Warren's trophies were two fine stag-heads, which had a place in the dining-room. He had to tell Rob more than once how they were shot, and to answer many a question about the difficulties and methods of deer-hunting. Rob had added a repeating-rifle to his armament, and he practised a good deal with it at a mark until he had become quite expert in this use of it. His cousin warned him, however, that it was one thing to hit a target, and another to hit a deer running in the woods, even if he escaped an attack of "buck fever."

Rob was delighted when his cousin, on reading a letter one evening in the following summer, told him that he had an invitation to pass ten days with a friend at his camp in the Adirondacks, and that he thought of accepting it, and taking Rob with him. Rob declared that this would be the greatest outing that he could imagine. He had read Murray's

"Adventures in the Wilderness," and gotten from this a vivid idea of the many attractions of the New York North Woods, and his cousin now gave him some of the reports of Verplanck Colvin to read on the same subject. So, when they started, he had a fair idea of the geography of the region.

The time of their trip was September. Taking the cars to Plattsburg, they went a short distance farther by rail to Au Sable Forks, where they took seats in a four-horse coach, with an all-day's ride before them. This was before the railroad had penetrated the wilderness, and driven the coaches away, so that Rob's first view of the big woods was not spoiled by that evidence of advancing civilization. The ride itself was an experience to him. They had seats with the driver, who was a jolly, talkative fellow, and had an endless supply of deer-hunting and fishing stories with which to entertain the boy. The road was a fairly good one, and the scenery became wilder as they advanced, and some of the noted mountains came into view; and Rob was sorry when the driver told him that another half-hour would land them on the shore of the Upper Saranac Lake, where they would take boats for the camp.

They found the boats of their friend awaiting them, and just as the evening shades were falling they set off for the upper end of the lake. There was no moon, but the stars were bright, and as they were rowed along the wooded shore they got at once the spirit of the wilderness.

Suddenly, after a row of several miles, a surprise was in store for them. Rounding a point along the shore, all at once they saw before them a little fairyland—trees hung with Chinese lanterns, a camp-fire sending up its bright flame and sparks, and a bombardment of Roman candles, mingled with cries of welcome. Rob had formed his idea of a camp in the woods as something quite different. The woods are now full of imitation "camps"—permanent cottages, supplied with all home luxuries, and attended by as large a corps of servants as is a city mansion. Mr. Warren's friend, Mr. Lewery, had not spoiled the wilderness in this way, but he had his family with him, and had done what was necessary for their comfort, without destroying the attractions of actual camp-life, and he had planned a little Fourth-of-July reception for his guests.

All lived in tents, but the tents had wooden floors,

Home Camp in the Adirondacks.

camp-cots, and the protection of "flies" to keep out the rain. Just back of the living-tents was the dining-tent, and back of this a tent in which the guides had their quarters. Near by, with a high rock as a backing, was the big camp-fire, round which some rustic seats were arranged, so that the fire could be enjoyed with the greatest comfort.

Rob was told that one of the guides, named Rollo, was to be his special attendant, and they became good friends at once. Rollo informed him that he liked boys if they did just as he told them to, did not scratch his boat in getting in and out, and were careful with their rifles. "You do as I tell you," he said to Rob, "and I'll eat my dog if we don't kill a deer."

Several days were devoted to visiting the friends in the camp, and making some little excursions in the neighborhood. Rob found that an Adirondack boat was a much more pretentious one than he had expected to find in the wilderness. Made of cedar, and kept carefully varnished, every guide looked on his own as possessing some advantage above those of his fellows, and Rob easily understood why he was cautioned about entering and leaving it with care. On the stern seat was a legless chair, with a round back, and, seated in this, with the guide as oarsman, the occupant could enjoy the scenery with the utmost comfort.

Finally it was announced that the two gentlemen and Rob, each with a guide, would start the next morning for a hunting trip of several days, leaving the ladies and the home-camp in charge of two other guides and the cook, who, by the way, was also a woodsman. Their course was to be up the lake for half a mile, then across "Cary's Carry," some two miles long, to the Raquette River, down this until Big Tupper Lake was reached, and then by Bog River and some more "carries" to a point near Little Tupper Lake, where they were to pitch their tent. The guides were busy the evening before, getting everything in readiness. As there would be considerable walking on the "carries," it was necessary to make their equipment as light as possible, but some things they must have. "Don't forget the axe." "Be sure you put in a lantern." "Take that bag of flour in your boat." These were some of the commands that might have been overheard as the guides were at work. Rob asked as few questions as possible, but there were a good many problems that presented themselves to him for solution. The morrow would supply the answers.

After an early breakfast, the little procession of three boats started on its way up the lake, with waving of handkerchiefs from the shore and promises of venison on the part of the departing sportsmen. The beginning of the "carry" was soon reached, and Rob then discovered the meaning of the term, and how the difficulty of getting over dry land with a boat was surmounted.

When the boats were drawn up to the shore, all got out, and the camp-supplies—provisions, frying-pans, axes, etc., with the oars and rifles, were distributed between Rob and his two friends. Then the guides fixed a wooden yoke across each boat, to distribute the weight, and each lifting his boat above his head, rested the yoke on his shoulders, and away they went. While the boats were lightly built, the weight for a two-mile "carry" was not insignificant, but the guides were sturdy fellows, and they trudged along steadily with their loads. Rob carried his rifle and as many of the oars as he could manage.

Two of the party who have not been mentioned were two deer-hounds. At this time, hounding deer was still permitted in the Adirondacks, and two of the guides were the owners of the hounds. They were lank animals, by no means so handsome as the bird-dogs at home, and their principal training had been to teach them to run on the track of a deer, and to pay no attention to the rabbits, of which there were many in the woods. Rollo owned one of the dogs, and he had a good deal to tell Rob as they rowed along about his efficiency.

At the end of the " carry " they came to the bank of the Raquette River, where the boats were launched again. This was a slow-moving stream, with wooded banks, its attractiveness being marred by the fact that the water, backed some years previously by a dam, had killed many of the trees. As Rob's boat, which was in advance, rounded a turn four wild ducks flew up. Rollo said they were shell-drakes, a narrow billed duck which fed on fish and were " poor eating." Rob put shells in a gun of Rollo's which was in the boat, in the hope of getting a shot at them, but they were not seen again.

Big Tupper Lake was reached about noon, and they landed at Moodie's, a once famous hunter's resort, and ate their lunch. Big Tupper Lake is a large body of water, and it was somewhat rough, but by skirting the windward shore they kept the boats dry. Reaching the upper end, two of the guides were sent to a house there to buy some potatoes, but none were to be had. This was a disappointment, as they had brought along a very small supply, in order to decrease their load.

From the lake the boats passed over a short "carry" into Bog River, a narrow but beautiful stream, which affords good trout-fishing earlier in the season, and about four o'clock they reached the place where it was proposed to stop. There they landed, and, unloading the tent and camp equipages, began the preparation of the camp. While the guides were putting up the tent and arranging a fire, the two elder hunters and Rob undertook the task of bed-making. Rob found that his idea of a bed of boughs was very crude. He had supposed that limbs of evergreen trees were simply cut and strewn on the ground, but his cousin told him that that kind of a bed would not do for him. First they cut down several small balsam-trees, and from these chopped off the branches. Inside the tent, when it was pitched, these branches were arranged in a slanting position, from the head down, so that when the bed, which occupied the whole tent space, was finished, it made a springy mattress. Over this, rubber blankets were first spread, and then woollen ones, and when all was arranged, the hunters had a sleeping-place which no one could complain of.

By the time all this work was completed it was dark, and the guides got supper. Rollo, who prided himself on his cooking skill, made hot biscuits, and they had fried bacon and potatoes, and fared well. Afterward, while the men smoked around a big camp-fire, Rob asked questions, and got some information about deer-shooting. He wanted to know if there were any dangerous wild animals in the woods, and was told that the wilderness lacked the element of danger, except the danger of getting lost, but that this could be accomplished very easily. "There ain't one guide in ten," said Rollo, "that dare go far enough into the thick woods to put out hounds as they ought to be.

You've got to take the dogs far enough in to let them get a good trail, and most of these guides that take out city parties would never find camp if they went half a mile from the 'carry.' You can get lost easier than you can do anything else in the big woods, and don't you forget it."

"But will not a compass guide them?" asked Rob.

"Not unless you know how to use one, and have the lay of the country in your mind. Once get turned round where you can't see anything but the sky above you, and your compass will tell you only that you don't know how you've been travelling. I laid a compass down one day on a stump, just to see which way it would point, when I was sure I knew my course, and I'm scorched if it did not tell me to go the other way. First I thought I would not, and then I said, 'Well, I'll give you a trial,' and I followed the compass's course for a mile and came out in a clearing I was after. There's one thing sure: if you use a compass you've got to mind it."

Suddenly Rob was startled by an unearthly sound coming from the woods near by. All laughed to see him jump, and they asked him if he was ready to tackle a wild-cat. Then Rollo explained that the sound was the hooting of a big owl. So the evening passed, and about nine o'clock all " turned in," and Rob slept like a top.

After an early breakfast the plans for the day's hunt were put in operation. Rollo was inclined to have Rob take a boat on a small lake near by, into which he was very sure the dogs would drive a deer; but the boy had heard so much condemnation from his cousin of the shooting of deer by rowing up to them and butchering them, that he said he would rather get no shot than to secure one in that manner. Both the elder hunters felt the same way; so each was placed by the guides on a runway—a place where deer when started would be likely to pass—and then Rollo set out into the woods with the hounds.

Rob's position was on a neck of land connecting a small lake with a slough, and he was warned not to get the "fever" if he heard the dogs giving tongue in his direction, for the deer would be ahead of them. Rob found a stump, with a big tree in front of it, and on this stump he took his seat to await events. He made a good many plans about the manner in which he would act if the deer came in sight, and he had plenty of time to do so, as not a sound of a dog reached his ear for two hours. He had some visitors, however. Once a partridge came out of the brush quite near him, and walked to the water and took a drink. This gave him a fine opportunity to observe the beauty of the bird. Then he heard a loud call in a tree-top, and got sight of a pileated woodpecker, the next to the largest of its species, known in the North as "cock of the woods." These birds were in earlier years abundant all over the Northern States, but are rare now, and he was fortunate to get a good look at one. It was as large as a teal duck, and its red topknot rendered it easily distinguishable among the branches.

So time passed, and Rob was deep in his thoughts when all at once the baying of a hound reached his ears. It was distant, but he had been told that if he heard the sound he could be sure that it came from one of their hounds, as no other hunters were in that region. So he got off his stump, and took his stand behind the big tree. The sound continued, sometimes at intervals, but after a time it certainly grew nearer. How his heart beat. Would he get the "fever" and be laughed at if he had a shot and missed? No. He would not miss. He would remember that Rollo had told him that if he gave a whistle the deer would probably stop a moment to locate the sound, and at that moment he would fire. In fact, he gave himself a lot of good advice.

Presently the baying came so near that he expected to see the deer at any moment, and then the direction changed, and soon he heard a rifle.

Someone else had got the shot.

An hour later Rollo was heard approaching through the woods, making noise enough with his mouth to render it certain that Rob would not mistake him for a deer. He said that the deer which his hound had started had turned back, and came only near enough to Mr. Lewery to give him a rather long snap-shot, which did not kill. That, however, would have to end their attempt that day. Rob and Rollo ate their lunch before starting for the camp, and found all the rest of the party there when they reached it. Mr. Lewery said that he got a good if brief look at the deer, which was a large doe, affording Rob some consolation in the thought that he had not lost a chance to kill a buck with antlers.

Soon came an aggravation. Three boats approached, with a party of tourists, and in one of the boats was the deer which, the guides said, was without doubt the one their hound had started. This party were not out for sport at all, but as they neared the upper end of Big Tupper one of their guides saw a deer swimming across a little bay, and he got near enough to it to allow one of the passengers to shoot it with the guide's rifle. Rollo, looking it over carefully, found a bullet-mark on its rump, and he said that that was undoubtedly made by Mr. Lewery. But the deer was too far in advance of the dogs to allow the Lewery party to claim it, and they had to swallow their disappointment.

"Blame the deer," said Rollo. "We gave it a gentlemanly chance to be killed in a sportsmanlike way, and what does it do but take to water in front of them tenderfeet, who could not hit a barn door if they did not stand on top of it. But we'll have to pot-hunt pretty soon, 'cause the taters is most gone, and we've got only one meal of ham."

In fact, their provisions were pretty low, because they had counted on getting a deer the first day. That evening Rob took a little walk up the stream, while supper was cooking, and, looking through the bushes, he spied a flock of several ducks. Hastening back, he loaded Rollo's gun, and saying nothing, slipped off to attempt to get a shot at them. When he reached the place where he had seen them they were not there, but he found them not far beyond, swimming slowly down the stream. The bushes on either side were thick, and he crept in their cover until he got within easy distance. As there was no chance of a shot after they took wing, he waited until he saw three heads in line, and then he fired. Breaking his way to the bank, he found all three of the ducks floundering in the water, and soon had them gathered and was on his way to camp. His cousin met him before he got there, having missed the boy, and started to see what the shot meant.

"No starvation now, Cousin Dave," cried Rob, holding up his ducks at arm's length.

"Well, you did get a shot, without mistake. Did you kill them all at once?"

Rob explained his exploit, and Mr. Warren told

him the ducks were greater mergansers (the bigger shelldrake), also called goosanders. They were fish-eaters, and not delicacies for the table, but he thought, in view of their commissary condition, they would try them. So, when the camp was reached, Rob and one of the guides picked them, and Rollo tried his hand at broiling them. Now, one of the things they had forgotten, in spite of all warnings, was a lantern, and the broiling and eating were done in the dark. Mr. Warren declared, notwithstanding Rollo's protests, that his piece of duck had not been near the fire, and Rob confessed that his needed pounding to enable him to get his teeth into it. But the meal made a good deal of sport, if it did not satisfy the palate, and Rob was told that he would have to dine on duck the next day if he did not kill a deer.

The weather was much cooler the next morning, and there was a little ice on the water-pail when they got up. The guides declared that it was an ideal day for deer, and the arrangement of the day before was renewed, except that Rollo let one of the other men put out the dogs, and he stayed with Rob. "I mean," said he (he had taken a great liking to the boy), "to have you kill a deer, and I believe I will be good luck."

There was again long waiting, and much complaint by Rollo about the course he supposed the guide with the hounds had taken (no one could do that work quite to his own satisfaction), and it was after ten o'clock when first a dog was heard to give tongue. Then the sound came from beyond Bog River, and Rollo said that the deer, if it came to them, would take the water from behind them. So they changed their station a little, giving them a wider view of the little lake in front. "Likelier'n not," said Rollo, "the deer will enter the water up the lake, but we must take our chances. I wish he would leap over that log out there. If he *should*, you must fire first, and I'll follow if you don't down him."

Deer often do the unexpected, and this one did. While Rob was listening to the still distant dogs, Rollo heard a crackling of brush in the woods, and whispered, "Now ready, by gum that deer's right on us." As he spoke, the deer broke out of the cover, and stopped to look around, right on the border of the lake, some seventy-five yards from where they stood. Before it had discovered them, Rob's rifle was at his shoulder, and he fired. The deer fell.

To do justice to Rob's feelings would be impossible. Rollo declared at the camp-fire that night that he did get the "fever," but that it came after the shot. Throwing down his rifle, he ran to the deer, and shouted, "O, Rollo, it's a buck, and it has got horns."

"Little ones," replied Rollo, with twinkling eye.

"They're big enough," said Rob. "I am going to have them set up, and send them to father for the dining-room at home."

It was indeed a young buck of fair size, with a pretty pair of antlers, and the boy had made a good shot, right behind the shoulder. He was allowed to admire it as long as he wanted to, and Rollo then handed Rob his rifle, and, tossing the deer across his shoulders, they set out for camp. When the rest of the party, who had been stationed farther away, came in, the deer was nicely hung on a limb, and Rob received the praise and congratulations that were his due.

Rob had learned that deer-hunting differed in

one important particular from bird-hunting. When the dogs had started a deer and its fate was decided one way or the other, that ended the day's hunt. The dogs were tired, and their baying had driven out of reach any other deer that might have been in the immediate neighborhood. Mr. Warren did not conceal his preference for bird-hunting, if only the sport was concerned, but said that he so loved the woods and the out-door life that there was charm enough for him in the wilderness, even if there had been no deer to hunt.

They stayed in this camp two more days, on one of which the two elder sportsmen went still-hunting with their guides, that is, without the dogs, leaving Rob to pass the day with Rollo. The dogs could not be put out, because they would have interfered with the sport of the others, and Rollo proposed to hunt for partridges, a plan to which Rob eagerly agreed. They were to take one rifle and one shotgun, and to use the rifle if any birds were treed.

Pocketing a lunch, they set out across Bog River, Rollo knowing the country in all that region very thoroughly. They were handicapped by having no dog, but Rollo was partridge-wise, and in a little swamp he put up a half-dozen birds at once. As soon as they rose he began barking like a dog, and several of the birds took to the trees. Rollo continued his barking, and Rob advanced within good rifle-shot, and took off the head of his first bird in good style. Rollo brought down one that Rob could not see because of the leaves, and Rob got one more, and then they continued their tramp, Rollo declaring his belief that the other hunters would have to look to them for supper.

There was a growth of hard wood—that is, beach and hickory—ahead of them, and Rollo suggested that they might get a shot at a gray squirrel there. A beech-tree stood on the border of this growth, and Rollo was telling Rob how fond bears were of beech-nuts when the boy exclaimed, "O, Rollo, what is that black thing over there?"

Rollo looked, and behold, a small black bear was taking itself into the farther swamp as fast as its legs could carry it, evidently much more afraid of man than any man was of it. "Shoot," said Rollo, and Rob, who had not remembered to do so sooner, fired into the bushes, but when they looked there, no bear was to be found. Rob was delighted to have even seen a bear, and said he could forgive himself for not shooting more quickly. Rollo, on his part, admitted that he did not discover the bear till Rob called his attention to it, but was sure that if his dog Esop had been with them the bear " would have had no show."

There were plenty of " workings," that is, shells of beech-nuts which squirrels had eaten, but no squirrels were to be seen, Rollo explaining that they did their feeding early and late in the day; but he discovered a clump of leaves in the upper branches of a tree, and said that this was a squirrel's nest, and that he would fire into it with his shotgun and see what would come out. He did so, and out sprang a fine gray squirrel, which he brought down with the second barrel. That ended their squirrel-shooting.

A long tramp failed to discover any more partridges until they came to an old wood road, made many years previously by timber-cutters. Following this, Rollo in advance, they reached a little brook, spanned by the remains of a bridge of logs. When he came in sight of this, Rollo dropped on his knees and held up his hand to Rob as a caution. " What is it?" asked Rob. " Look on that bridge," said Rollo. "A whole bunch of partridges, sunning themselves."

Rob saw them at once, and an interesting sight they were. Perhaps no foot of man had ever disturbed them, and they wallowed in the dust and pecked themselves, just like a flock of chickens in a barnyard. It would have been easy to kill a good many of them with one load of shot, but Rob would have not been so unsportsmanlike, and Rollo did not propose it. (What he might have done had he been alone I do not undertake to say.) When they had viewed the birds as long as they cared to, Rob proposed to try for the big cock-bird's head, with the rifle, and to let Rollo chance his luck with the gun when the birds got up. Rollo was no wing-shot, but he did not say so. Rob awaited his opportunity, and, firing at what seemed to be the father of the flock, decapitated him nicely. Rollo let the others have both barrels of his shotgun, but without effect. He afterward declared that the sun shone in his eyes and spoiled his aim. There are various ways of accounting for misses.

Soon after this they turned their steps homeward—so Rollo said; Rob had not an idea of their locality—finding the woods, which were rather open, quite devoid of game. Presently a steep ridge rose before them, up which they trudged in single file. Stopping to rest on its summit, Rollo was pointing out the direction of the camp to Rob, when both saw at once a small doe running leisurely in the valley beneath them. It did not see nor wind them, but it was too far off to shoot, and there was no chance of creeping up to it in such open woods; so they stood still and admired it until it disappeared. Rob said that what surprised him most was its apparent smallness. He had expected to see every deer stand up as large as a cow, and this one was not apparently bigger than a good-sized dog. Rollo told him that this was the common experience of those who had their first sight of deer, and he instanced the case of a young man with whom he stood on a run-way, and who thought a deer that came out by them was a dog, and did not shoot before it had darted back again.

The rest of the party had reached camp when they got there, and Mr. Warren and his guide had brought in a fine doe. Rob was almost as much delighted in hearing the story of its capture as he would have been in killing it himself. Indeed, he had honestly wished that his cousin might kill the next deer. It seemed that on coming to a rising piece of woods, with a swampy growth on one side of it, the guide had placed Mr. Warren where the ridge sloped off to the south of the swamp, and had then acted as dog, and entered the swamp at the other end. By good luck a deer was feeding in the swamp, and by some more good luck it took a course within range of the rifle, and Mr. Warren dropped it dead.

"Was it moving when you shot, Cousin Dave?" asked Rob. He was told that it was going on a gentle lope. "Then," said he, "you are a little ahead of me, for my deer had stopped when I fired."

"But," interposed Rollo, "yours is a buck."

They let that settle the question, and listened with interest to Rob's story of seeing the bear, Mr. Lewery declaring that to shoot a bear was now his ungratified ambition, and Rollo offering to guarantee him a shot at one if he would prolong his stay until December.

On the other day of their stay no deer came

within sight or shot of either of the party, and the next morning the home-trip was begun, and the home-camp was duly reached without any incident of note on the way. The hunters had lived on venison and biscuit for two days, their vegetables having given out, and the whole camp had a royal supper that night, of which venison chops and broiled partridges were the features.

CHAPTER VIII

DUCK-SHOOTING ON BARNEGAT BAY

TWO or more years later (we need not be particular about the years any longer) a November afternoon found Rob and his cousin in the cars, on the way to Barnegat, New Jersey, where they were to enjoy a few days' sport with the wild ducks. Rob had listened with great interest to many a talk by his cousin about this sport, of which Mr. Warren was very fond, and his expectations of a grand time were aroused to the highest point.

When they stepped on the platform of the depot at Barnegat village, a little man whose face, except a pair of bright eyes, was concealed by a thick growth of whiskers, greeted Mr. Warren warmly, and was introduced to Rob as Jesse Birdwell, the bayman who would provide the boats and be their cook and general director during their stay. No time was lost in the preliminary arrangements. While Mr. Warren and Rob ate their supper at the hotel, Jesse did the marketing for the trip. They would live on his yacht, without visiting the mainland until the shooting was ended, and it was necessary therefore to take all their stores with them. Mr. Warren simply gave Jesse a bill, with the instruction, "Get what is necessary," and he knew they would not come short.

After supper Jesse met them in a ramshackle old stage which was to convey them and their shooting-equipment and supplies to the bay, something over a mile distant. Arriving there, the visitors waited on an old dock until Jesse brought up his yacht. The yacht, while comfortable in every way, and a fine sailing craft, was devoid of the elegances and comforts that are supposed to mark a yacht's equipment. The cabin was small, and contained only common lockers, a seat running around it, a little stove astern the centreboard, a table, that was let down by the side of the centreboard when not in use, and some mattresses. When the hatch was pulled over, a man could not stand up in the cabin, but as they used the boat only at night, and as there was a folding-chair to accommodate Mr. Warren, he declared that he did not want any-

DUCK-SHOOTING ON BARNEGAT BAY

thing better. The true sportsman knows that luxuries and success with game do not often go together.

When Jesse had stowed away his stores to his satisfaction, the sail was raised, and they stood across the bay. Jesse told Mr. Warren where he proposed to spend the night, but all that Rob understood about it was that it would be within easy reach of the shooting-ground.

Behind the yacht trailed three small boats, which were really the most essential part of their equipment, and about which a few descriptive words are necessary. As Barnegat Bay is a big piece of water, the native wild-fowl shooter, who for generations has followed the business for a living in the proper seasons, finds it necessary to have a sail-boat big enough to render it safe for him to cross the bay, and go in any direction, no matter how rough the weather may be. But wild fowl are very wary birds, and it would be folly to attempt to approach them in a big boat carrying a mast and sail. Something has to be provided, therefore, from which to do the shooting, when the neighborhood of the shooting-ground is reached.

Out of this necessity was evolved the small gunning-boat known as the "Barnegat sneak-box." The sneak-box (a name derived from its use in sneaking on the birds) is a keel-boat, generally 12 feet in length, about 3 feet and 7 inches in width, and 10 inches in depth amidship. It is partly decked over, like a canoe, has a movable mast and a centreboard, and is also equipped with movable rowlocks and oars. Perhaps no boat of its size was ever built that can sail closer to the wind, and that can "live" in rougher water, when it is sailed by a man who knows how to get out of it its best work. When the gunner is ready to go for ducks or geese, he leaves his bigger boat at anchor a mile or more from his shooting-ground, and does his shooting from his sneak-box, which not only carries him just where he wants to go, but, when arrived there, affords him a perfect place of concealment.

Rob enjoyed the sail across the bay very much, although the air was keen, and Jesse good-naturedly answered his many questions—explaining how the appearance and disappearance of the light in the light-house toward which they were sailing permitted the sailors on the ocean to identify it, telling him more than I have told about the sneak-boxes, in whose sailing qualities he had the greatest faith, and predicting some good sport if the weather did not turn mild. He said that there were plenty of ducks in the bay, but that on still, warm days they were usually quiet on their feeding-grounds, while in rougher weather they kept moving, and thus came within sight of the decoys.

The anchorage-ground being reached, Jesse put out a small anchor from both the fore and aft part of the boat, saying that he could not sleep well if the boat was swinging around all night. Next he insisted on lighting his stove and making them a cup of coffee, which they accepted, and then he said that they would better get ready for bed, as he would have them up betimes in the morning. "How early?" asked Rob. "It's sun-rise about half-past six," Jesse replied, "and we want to be rigged out before that hour. So, as I have to be cook and house-maid at the same time, you will hear me stirring about half-past three." Rob concluded that the advice about turning in early was good.

The sleeping accommodations of the Florence (so the yacht was named) were primitive. For Mr.

Warren, Jesse made a bed by placing two springy boards on two wooden "horses," and covering the boards with a mattress. "You'll have to sleep with me," said he to Rob. "The Florence does not expect two guests at once." Sleeping with Jesse meant creeping forward where there were two other mattresses, and covering up with some blankets, without removing more than his outer garments. But Rob took to his quarters readily, and was soon lulled to sleep by the lapping of the water against the side of the boat.

The first thing that he was conscious of the next morning was the sound of a sizzling frying-pan, and the odor of frying ham. "Breakfast 'most ready," said Jesse. "Time to get up. You don't have much dressing to do." As their fresh-water keg was not a large one, Rob was advised to dip up a bucket of the bay water for his ablutions, Jesse laughingly recommending it for his complexion. It was cold and cloudy and dark as pitch when he stuck his head out of the cabin—a likely morning for ducks, Jesse observed.

They sat down to a breakfast of fried ham and eggs, boiled potatoes, bread and butter and coffee, all nicely prepared, and all cooked on what Jesse called his "two-holed stove." "Save some appetite before you finish," said their cook. "Why, is there another course?" asked Rob. "Sure," said Jesse; "I can always shoot better on buckwheat cakes;" and buckwheat cakes they had, and good ones, too, made from Jesse's self-raising flour, and topped off with maple syrup. Rob thought to himself that if Jesse's shooting was measured by the cakes he ate, a great day was before them, for he had never seen such a pile of them disappear as did in front of the bayman.

Breakfast finished, Jesse "did up his work," as he called it. This consisted of throwing overboard every scrap of the remnants, and washing the dishes. "Two things I won't do," said he. "One is to have any left-over things in my pantry, and the other is to have any washing up to do when I come in at night. Do all the work before you start, and then you can enjoy the day."

And now came what Rob was waiting for, the start for the shooting-ground. Mr. Warren asked no questions about this and gave no suggestions, for he knew that Jesse would bring to the solution of the matter years of experience, and a perfect knowledge of the bay. First, each sneak-box was relieved of the wooden hatch that keeps out the rain when it is not in use, the hatches being placed on the deck of the yacht. Each gunner then placed in his box the things he would want to use. Mr. Warren and Rob had each a rubber blanket and an air-pillow, besides their guns and cartridge-boxes. Jesse's oil-skin coat served him instead of a rubber blanket, and a bunch of marsh hay did for his pillow.

"Can you row, Rob?" he asked at the start. "Some," said Rob, "but I do not call myself an oarsman." "I'll give you a tow," said Jesse. "We've got a goodly pull ahead of us, for I always want to be a safe distance from any mast that might steer off the birds." Accordingly, he tied the painter (tie-rope) of Rob's boat to the stern of his, and, with Mr. Warren bringing up the rear, the procession moved on. A sneak-box is by no means a light boat, and Rob's arms got very tired long before Jesse announced that their rowing was nearly over.

It was still very dark when they started, and for

some time the only object Rob could discover was the light-house light, to their right. After a while the beach became dimly visible, and Rob noticed that they passed several points of land that jutted out into the bay. In skirting one of these Jesse called out to Mr. Warren, "Remember killing the two geese off that point there?" "Don't I!" replied Mr. Warren. "I had you there, Jesse."

Rob asked no questions at the time, but he mentally saved up some.

After more than half an hour of this progress, Jesse stood up in his boat and, taking a good look around, remarked, "We're pretty near about right now." Moving the boat as he stood with one oar as a paddle, he scanned the surface of the water, and presently cried, "Whoa. Here's the place." Rob now stood up, too, and looked around him. Then he was puzzled. Instead of being along the shore, as he supposed they would be when they should stop in preparation for the shooting, they were half a mile from any land, out in the bay, on the beach side. What added to his bewilderment was the fact that the sneak-boxes were painted white, and he could not see why a wary duck could not discover them quite as easily as it could the yacht which Jesse was so anxious to leave far behind. But he decided to await results, and not unveil his curiosity too soon.

Jesse understood, however, that the boy must be somewhat at a loss to understand the situation, and he said, as he drew from his boat a long-handled rake with very curved teeth, "I'll soon have some work for you and Mr. Warren to do. I suppose you think this is a queer place in which to hide for ducks." Rob confessed that he did. "We might shoot from points, and we often do," Jesse continued. "When I size up a city man who comes down here with a twelve-bore gun and a lot of cigarettes, and does not know a canvas-back from a coot, I put that man on a point, no matter how the wind is and what the weather. If I took all the trouble to rig out in such a place as this, he couldn't hit anything if it came along, and he would not keep his head below deck, and he would want to go to the yacht for dinner at noon. I've had plenty of that sort. But your cousin knows good ducks, and won't shoot poor ones, and he knows how to shoot, and, seeing that we are two to one against you, you can't leave here till we get ready."

During this conversation Jesse had been drawing up with his rake great masses of sea-weed, whose location had been revealed to him by a fleck of foam on the surface of the water that indicated the presence of the weed beneath. This foam was the discovery that decided the precise location of their stopping-place. The weed was drawn by him away from the centre, so as to leave an open place into which the others were told to shove their boats. Then another puzzle was explained to Rob. The sneak-boxes were, as we have seen, painted white, and Jesse asked his companions to cover their decks with the weed while he was putting out the stools. This was really not very pleasant work, for the weeds were cold and slimy and gritty, and Rob was quite chilled before he got through.

Finally he asked: "Cousin Dave, why do the baymen not paint these boats the color of the banks and the weeds, and save all this bother of covering them with the sea-weed?"

"Because the baymen, when they shoot for market in the winter, as they do, use their boats on the ice. When the bay is nearly frozen over, there are large air-holes, and into these many ducks drop to feed. The baymen push their boats to the edge of a convenient air-hole, pile up some cakes of ice around them, put out some stools, and often kill a large number of birds in a day. Few visiting sportsmen try this kind of shooting, as it is cold, rough work. Now, to conceal a boat in the ice, the boat must be white. One of any other color could not be concealed by ice-cakes. On the other hand, you see that it requires only a little disagreeable work to conceal a white boat with sea-weed right out in the bay or on a point. When Jesse has done with our dressing, not many ducks will know us from a bunch of sea-weed such as are to be seen all over the flats at low water."

The color of the sneak-boxes was no longer a puzzle.

Meanwhile Jesse was busy putting out the decoys that he had carried, piled up on the forward part of his boat. There were about fifty of these, representing ducks of different kinds, with a few brant. Mr. Warren told Rob that Jesse made all his own decoys, and that they were much better than any for sale in the stores—all hollow, of cedar, and so ballasted with lead underneath that they rode with the closest imitation to the live birds. Rob was cautioned by his cousin, and later by Jesse, not to fire at a duck while it was among the decoys, because it would break Jesse's heart to have any of the latter filled with shot-holes and made leaky.

Each decoy was fastened to a weight by a cord, and Jesse cast them overboard rapidly, so distributing them that when he was through with the work, the imitation had the most natural appearance of a flock of real birds resting on the water. Mr. Warren pointed out that their boats lay so that the wind blew from them to the decoys. The decoys were placed in this way because ducks always come up against the wind in lighting on the water, and this arrangement would both place the decoys between the birds and the boats when they came toward the stools, and would give the gunners the best opportunity to shoot. Thus was Rob initiated into some of the lore of duck-shooting.

Finally all their preparations had been made. Jesse placed his boat on the right, with Rob's next, and Mr. Warren's to the left. Every uncovered spot on the boats was detected and concealed under the bayman's direction. The boats contained marsh hay, and when the hunters were stretched out on their backs, with their air-pillows under their heads, and their blankets spread over them, they were as comfortable as could be desired.

"Now," said Jesse to Rob, "the one thing to be remembered above all others is to keep close. I have more trouble to get city men to do this than I do to get birds for them, for if they will keep down I can shoot the birds myself. We are a bunch of sea-weed now to the birds if our heads do not stick up, but if they do, the birds will suspect right away, and have no use for us. Bend the brim of your hat down over your eyes, and merely peep over the stern of the boat. Just like that," he added, as Rob settled himself down.

Rob found many things to interest him as they awaited the coming of day. On the mainland here and there a little column of smoke would show itself, indicating preparations for an early breakfast. To the south a few sails were noticed, belonging to baymen who would probably try their luck on the main shore. A little house on the ocean side of the beach, partly visible, was pointed out to Rob as the life-saving station of that district. High in the air flies a swift-winged bird, the first they have seen—a loon, greatest of divers, but not classed as a game-bird at all. "What are those birds to the right, away out in the bay?" "Ducks, but not coming our way." Broad-bills, Jesse thinks, but the light is poor still. A low-flying bird is coming straight up the bay. Yes, it sees the stools. "Head down, Rob, it is coming in. No, don't get ready to shoot. It is a saw-bill (Jesse's name for shelldrake) and no good." "Test your nerve on it," says Cousin Dave, "and say bang when you would shot." "Bang," as the bird swings up into clear view. "Sit up and look at it, and see how your shot would have told." Rob finds that the bird was at least seventy-five yards distant, when he thought it was so near that he could blow it to pieces. "Nothing so deceptive as shooting over the water." He is never to shoot at a flock until Jesse gives the word.

"Down close," from Jesse. "There is a bunch that ought to see us. Yes, they do, broad-bills. Pick out your bird before you shoot, and take the middle of the flock, Rob. Your cousin will take some of the leaders and I will try at the rear birds. There are two dozen of them."

Every nerve in Rob's body thrilled. That mass of wings, that inrush of the big birds—and how big they looked—coming right at them, without a sound. Why does not Jesse say fire? Surely the birds are close on them. Jesse knows better, and so does Cousin Dave. The birds have seen the decoys, and the gunners can pick out their time to shoot. "Now," as they catch the wind and drop their feet, in expectation of lighting. At the word the three sit up, guns to shoulder, and there are three almost simultaneous reports. When Rob sat up the air in front of him seemed full of ducks, and his impulse was simply to fire into the flock. But a memory of that story of the Maryland quail came to him in time, and "pulling himself together," he aimed at one of the birds in front of him, and saw it go down just as Jesse cried, "Now steady with the other barrel;" but he did not bring down number two.

"The boy did well," said Jesse to Mr. Warren. "I guess the three of us will get some birds." It was Rob's test. Had he "gone to pieces" and

Duck-Shooting on Barnegat Bay.

brought down nothing, Jesse's interest in the trip would have been greatly decreased.

"How many did the rest of you get?" asked Rob.

"Two with my right and one with my left," said Jesse. "And you, Mr. Warren?"

"Two with each."

"Sure you ain't counting some of my birds?"

"Where are yours?"

"Just beyond the decoys. One of them is not dead yet."

"You can see mine between me and the beach. I shot when they had passed the point of the decoys."

There could be no dispute about birds so well distributed, and Jesse pushed out his boat and gathered them in. Eight birds out of the first flock was doing remarkably well, much better than they could expect to average.

Before they were settled again another flock, black ducks, Jesse said, came within sight, but changed their course. Several flocks were next seen crossing the beach from the ocean, but they had their minds fixed on some point up the bay, and did not come within sight of the stools. But those birds over there are surely coming. No, they have not seen the stools. They veer off toward the mainland. Jesse gives a call, and they seem to change their course. Then he throws his foot in the air, in imitation—a crude one, but sometimes effective—of a duck stretching its wings. Something tells, foot or call, for the birds have decided to see what that flock of apparent ducks have found to feed on so early. "Red-heads, for sure," whispered Jesse, as they came up. Seven only, but redheads. Rob got no direction this time how to shoot. It was "Now," when the birds swung over the stools, and the three guns cracked. Birds fell, but Rob did not know who had killed them, and the rest were so far to the right that he did not fire his second barrel. Jesse did and killed one, and Mr. Warren screwed himself round on his knees and took a long shot back of the boat, making his bird stagger, but not stopping it. Only three of the flock lay quiet among the stools. The elder sportsmen were self-critical about not bringing down more of them, explaining the result in several ways, but agreeing that they could have done much better if the birds had not kept so close together, and had spread out over the decoys. The killing of the three birds was not apportioned, but both the others said that it was fair that Rob should have the credit for one, as he was in the centre.

So the morning passed. The sky remained clouded and the air cool, but, in their boats, lying on the hay and with their blankets tucked over them, the sportsmen were very comfortable, Jesse even complaining of being too warm. There were almost always some ducks in sight, but by no means all of them came within shot. Rob "did himself proud," as Jesse put it, by bringing down a single mallard, the only one they saw. It was a beautifully marked duck, a species, Mr. Warren told him, more abundant on inland waters than along the coast.

About noon they ate their lunch, and while they were doing so Rob said, " What about the two geese you killed off the point we passed this morning, Cousin Dave?"

"That," said Mr. Warren, "was the only time I ever got the best of Jesse on the bay. It was a good many years ago, the first time I ever came down here in the spring for geese. I got to Barnegat one March evening, in a rain-storm. We stayed on the yacht in the creek during the night, and sailed across the bay early in the morning, anchoring about where we did last night. It still rained, and we did not go out during the forenoon; but about one o'clock the boat swung round, indicating a change of the wind, and Jesse told me to get on my rubber boots, predicting a movement of geese that afternoon. Before we had reached the point we passed this morning, several flocks of geese appeared, and we concluded to stop there, although Jesse wanted to shoot from a point a mile beyond, saying that the men from the life-saving station were very likely to go out on the point in front of their place to try for a shot, and, if they did so, they would turn the birds away from us. This was a good prediction, for the first two flocks that appeared after we got rigged out were shot at below us, and veered away. Presently a flock came into view out in the bay, and Jesse began honking to them. You have not heard Jesse honk yet. They do say that if a mother goose has a bird that is not a good honker she brings it within sound of Jesse to get a lesson. These geese heard Jesse's call, and they turned toward us. The tide had risen since we ran our boats ashore, and the sterns, toward the bay, were thus tipped up a little, concealing our decoys and the nearby water from us as we lay. Jesse, at that time, was shooting a big eight-gauge muzzle-loader, with which he thought he could bring down a goose at seventy-five yards.

"When the geese loomed up before us, apparently within range, Jesse cried, 'Give it to them,' and we both rose and pulled. Owing to our position, the birds were farther off than they had seemed to be, and neither of Jesse's shots told. Then came my luck. While Jesse had been out rearranging the stools, a few moments before these birds appeared, I had lowered the hammers of my gun, as a measure of safety, and when he returned I had forgotten to raise them. Therefore, when I pulled the triggers, neither barrel was discharged. But while we had been watching the birds in the flock, two of their number, flying low, had come in unobserved by us, and lit among the decoys. 'Shoot 'em, shoot 'em,' cried Jesse. Raising my hammers, I fired at each of them as they rose to fly, and both dropped. If my gun had been cocked, I, too, would have fired at the flock, and we would not have got a goose."

"I knew the birds were broad off," said Jesse, by way of excuse, "but I expected those life-saving fellows would shoot any minute, and so I got up too quick."

The afternoon flight was a fairly good one, and when, a little before sundown, the stools were taken up, there was a fine pile of ducks on the stern of their boats. The wind was in their favor, and Jesse put up the sail in his sneak-box, and taking the other two in tow, they were not long in reaching the yacht. The little stove was soon aglow, and Jesse served them a supper of beefsteak and boiled potatoes, with canned peas and coffee, to which they did full justice.

The shooting the next day was not so good, but they killed a fair number of birds. When Rob awoke the morning following, it was daylight. Jesse said that the sky was so clear and the air so warm that he did not think they would do much with the ducks, and so he had let them sleep. Mr. Warren proposed that he take his sneak-box to some point on the beach and try his luck alone, while Jesse and

DUCK-SHOOTING ON BARNEGAT BAY

Rob went off by themselves, two boats making less show in the water than three, and this was agreed to.

Jesse said there were a good many ducks feeding near the inlet, and he put out the stools as on the first morning, on a flat, about a mile from their feeding-ground. It was indeed a poor day for ducks. The sun was bright, and scarcely a ripple disturbed the surface of the bay. In such weather ducks feed at their leisure, and then sit and sun themselves till something disturbs them or their mood changes, and the hunter's chance is a poor one. For two hours they did not get a shot. Then Rob spied a single duck swimming half a mile away from them. Jesse "reckoned" that it was a black duck, but was not sure, and at any rate he did not count on getting a shot. But the tide slowly brought the bird toward them, and presently it was within gunshot—a big black drake. Rob said he should like to watch it, and he thought that it might prove a good decoy. Jesse let him have his way, and lo! the bird swam right up among the decoys and, tucking its head under its wing, went to sleep! "If that ain't impudence," said Jesse. "It don't show us the least bit of respect."

They let it sleep awhile, and then Jesse proposed that Rob scare it up, and shoot it, saying that perhaps that would bring them luck. So Rob stood up in his boat and shouted, and the amazed duck took wing, and was knocked down very cleanly. Jesse declared that there was no better "eating bird" than a black duck, and that half the persons who thought so much of canvas-backs and red-heads could not tell one of these from a black duck cooked in the same way.

Toward noon Jesse pointed out five large birds that were flying in a southerly course far out in the bay. "Those are brant," said he. "I wish you could get a shot at them, but you won't."

"What are brant?" asked Rob.

"The brant is a bird a good deal like a Canada goose, but smaller. Your cousin has told me that in some of the books it is called a brant goose, and that, in olden time, there was a belief that it was hatched from a barnacle shell which grew on water-soaked logs. But I guess it is hatched from a brant egg, sure enough. We kill a good many of them at times, and I think they are fine birds. Their necks are black, and they have a white mark

DUCK-SHOOTING ON BARNEGAT BAY

at their throats. A brant will weigh about four pounds. They are a stupid sort of bird, too. If a shot hits one, he seems to give right up, and lights on the water and hollers, while a goose will carry off half a load if it does not hit right. I do believe those birds are looking for company," and the bayman began to honk at them.

Rob had never heard a brant honk, but he was quite willing to accept Jesse's call as a correct one, and so were these birds, for, after circling round a little, they dropped lower down and then flew toward the stools. As they approached, Jesse said they ought to get them all, because, if they killed two apiece as they came in, the other one would not fly away. But the brant, instead of flying over the decoys as Jesse expected them to, came in close to the water, and dropped down right in the midst of the wooden ducks. "Don't shoot yet," said Jesse, his precious decoys in his mind. "We can choose our shots."

Rob now had a fine opportunity to study the shape and color of the birds. Presently two of them swam to one side of the decoys, and Jesse said, "If you can get those two heads in line, give it to them, and then we can shoot as they rise." Rob fired a moment later, and the two birds he aimed at on the water stayed there, while the others took wing. One of these fell wounded but not dead before Rob's second barrel. Jesse did not shoot. The generous-hearted bayman had seen that the birds were young ones, and, when the boy had done so well with his two shots, he determined to give him a chance to kill the other two. The latter flew off for some distance and lit in the bay. This was what Jesse expected.

"Now," said he, "I will row around those two birds, and they will come to stool again, and you must drop them both." His prediction was verified. When the two live brant took wing, they flew directly for the decoys, and, making an easy shot, Rob dropped one with each barrel. "Tell me that that black duck did not bring us luck," said Jesse. "Your cousin will have to do well to beat you to-day."

That ended their luck, however, for that day, except that they got three out of a bunch of broadbills in the afternoon. Jesse picked two of these, and gave them fricasseed duck for dinner, a dish on whose excellence he expatiated. Mr. Warren was on board the yacht when they arrived. He had had poor luck, but could show them one black duck, one red-head, and two broad-bills as his contribution.

When they said good-by to Jesse at the station, Rob declared that he had had a splendid time, and never wanted to shoot ducks with any other guide, and Jesse said that he had never broken in a young bay-shooter who had done so well the first time.

CHAPTER IX

QUAIL-SHOOTING IN NORTH CAROLINA

MR. WARREN had made several trips to North Carolina for quail-shooting before Rob became his companion, and one autumn he proposed a visit there, where he told Rob the birds were much more abundant than in the North. Besides, he said, it was interesting to become acquainted with new people and a new country, and he thought the trip would be an agreeable one, aside from the shooting.

North Carolina may be divided into three sections: the coast section (where the literal "tar heels," as North Carolinians are sometimes nicknamed, the turpentine-makers, dwell), a region of low swamps and big ditches; the middle section, flat and level, and without scenic attraction, but dryer; and the mountain section of the west. Their stopping-place was to be a village in the middle section, and at the station there one after-

QUAIL-SHOOTING IN NORTH CAROLINA

noon in November, they found Mose, an old darky who had waited on Mr. Warren many times, with a team of horses to convey them to the house of Mr. Bullis, a mile out of the town. Rob was told that Mose was a preacher of reputation among the colored people, and as efficient in noting the resorts of quail as he was in the pulpit.

At Mr. Bullis's house Rob found their quarters to be a big room in a cottage situated a hundred feet from the dwelling. There were two big beds in the room, and an enormous fireplace, in which Mose had a welcome fire burning. Mose declared that "partridges," as quails are called in the South, were "right smart plenty," and he predicted very good sport.

Before the sportsmen were out of bed the next morning, Mose had a fire lighted on the hearth, and promised them a fine day for hunting. Rob now had an illustration of the leisurely way in which Southern people do things. He and Mr. Warren were ready for their breakfast before seven o'clock, but the cook was not. Mr. Bullis came in to say that the meal would be ready "right away," but it was eight before they were called. Rob accounted for some of this delay when he saw the table. A Southern breakfast is not a breakfast without plenty of hot bread, and they had not only hot corn-bread of the kind he was acquainted with, but hot muffins, "egg-bread," which looked to him like a stiff pudding, and after these griddle-cakes. He concluded that if the cook had to make all these dishes every morning, there was a good reason why the meal was late. As Mr. Bullis was to accompany them, he was next waited for, and when Mose was sent to find out what delayed him, he returned with the word that "he was most through havin' prayers."

Finally, a little before nine o'clock, they moved off. They had brought with them two of their dogs, Rob's Cap and Mr. Warren's Dan, who was a fast ranger, and Mr. Bullis took with him a dog of his own training named Joe, who proved to be a wide ranger and to have a good nose, but who had about as much idea of minding his master as a spoiled child.

The territory through which they walked was flat, with a good deal of wood-land, interspersed with fields, many of them grown up with a grass

QUAIL-SHOOTING IN NORTH CAROLINA

called broom-sedge, which made excellent cover, and many of them cultivated with corn or cotton. Rob noticed that the soil was thin and sandy, and that only one stalk of corn grew in a hill, instead of the three or four to be found in the North. Most of the cotton had been picked, but enough still remained in the bolls to give him an idea of the appearance of a cotton field, and he saw during the day some groups of ragged rather than picturesque negroes at work picking.

Passing through a piece of open pine woods, they came to a "branch," as a gully through which a stream runs is called in that part of the country, and there, Mose assured them, "a big bunch of pa'tridges uses." "Uses" was Mose's term for having a feeding-ground. All the dogs were sent forward, and Joe took the lead, racing at a pace which led Rob to think that he would run over any birds he might come across. But although Joe was not trained as nicely as the Northern dogs, he knew his business, and, while Rob was watching him, he swung round to the wind, slowed his pace and then pointed toward a clump of grass. His owner, well pleased that his dog had found first, cried, "Joe's got 'em," and they all walked up to him. But before they got there, Cap, who was ranging to the left, pointed also.

"Well, Mose," said Mr. Warren, "the birds must be thick, if we are to have two points at once."

"I reckoned dey was right smart of 'em," chuckled Mose, taking the points half to his own credit.

Mr. Bullis thought that Cap might be pointing an "old hare" (a rabbit of any age is an "old hare" in North Carolina), but as Mr. Warren knew that Rob's dog would not break his point even when the men shot at another flock, he suggested that they see what Joe had first. Dan had run ahead of them and backed Joe, and they had a pretty sight as they advanced. It was evident from the stiffness of the dog that the birds were close at hand, and when the word "Hie on" was given, there was a whir of wings that almost upset Rob's nerve. It was indeed a fine flock that Joe had found, and they made direct for the cover of the woods. Rob dropped one and missed one, Mr. Warren dropped two, and Mr. Bullis "thought" that he killed the one he fired at, but the dogs did not discover it. They learned during the day that their host rarely missed, but that his luck in finding his birds was often poor. This became a source of amusement to his companions. "Ef de ole man could find as good as he can shoot," remarked Mose to Rob, "dere would be a pile of game in his pockets."

They now went to Cap to see what he was pointing, before following up the other birds. He still stood as stiff as a rod, pointing into a little growth of alders. "Step round that side," said Mr. Warren to Rob, "and be ready for a woodcock." This advice proved good, for, when the dog was sent forward, a fine cock rose and darted toward Rob. In spite of his warning, Rob missed it with his first barrel, but he downed it with the second. Mr. Warren told Rob that he had never found many woodcock in that neighborhood in November, but once killed a good many in February, birds on their way North. Mose expressed some doubts about the snipe, as he called it, being "a good eatin' bird," and was sorry that it had not proved to be one of the "old hares" which were his own great delicacy, after the possum, and which would have gone into his pocket.

The party now retraced their steps, to look for the scattered birds of the first flock. The woods ahead were quite open, but the pine needles underneath the trees made a poor cover, and only one bird was found by the dogs until they came again to the open. This proved to be a large field, uncultivated, and with a good deal of broom-sedge. Each dog had a point right away, and each hunter stepped up to his own dog. This time Mr. Bullis both killed and found his bird, and the other two were equally fortunate.

But the birds had scattered widely, and after spending some time in the field, and adding only one more to their bag, Mose said he knew where there was another flock nearby, and that it was not worth while to waste more time there. Mr. Warren accepted this advice, but he told Rob that it would not have been good at home, where there were fewer birds; for it was his experience in the North that the man who got the most birds was the one who stayed with a flock, once it was flushed, until there was no hope of finding more.

QUAIL-SHOOTING IN NORTH CAROLINA

In going through a low-lying corn-stubble, Rob had an opportunity to make the acquaintance of the Southern cockle-bur. It grows in wet places, and is hard, and as big as a man's thumb. Rob could easily imagine the plight of a setter with its hair matted with these burs. Presently, Mose asked him, "Do you like 'simmons?" Rob had never tasted them, so Mose led him to a tree, underneath which lay a quantity of the fruit, so ripe with the frost that almost every one was burst open. These were persimmons, a fruit that grows wild in the South as abundantly as do hickory-nuts and chestnuts in the North. Mose told him they were the "puckeriest" things imaginable till the frost ripened them. Rob found them very much to his taste, and he made his desert under a persimmon-tree every day during his stay, at the noon lunch. Mose also introduced him to the may-pop, the fruit of the passion flower. This was found in cultivated fields, resembling a tomato somewhat in appearance, and having a sweet and pleasant taste.

"Dey's birds hereabout, sure," said Mose, when they came to an open country, after passing through some woods. There were no cultivated fields in sight, only a big unfenced district, with plenty of cover in the shape of broom-sedge and weeds, and with open pine woods beyond. It looked like slow work to find birds in so much cover, and it would have been with slow dogs. But Joe and Dan were used to Southern hunting, and Cap was not to be left behind, and away the three went, quartering to right and left, and covering a big extent of territory in short order. Cap was the first to make game, slowing up and lashing his tail far out in the field. He trailed for some distance, the birds apparently having been feeding widely, as there was nothing but the weed-seeds for them to eat there. At last he pointed. Joe had come near enough to back him.

"Dis is mighty open shootin', gemmen," said Mose, laughing, "an' I counts on pickin' up six birds." But he did not "count" right. More than a dozen birds got up, but only four went down. Mr. Warren, with his cool head, almost always got two out of a flock, and did so this time. Mr. Bullis shot (and found) one, and Rob missed with his second barrel. "How is it, Cousin Dave," he asked, while the dogs were retrieving the birds, "that you kill two out of a flock so easily, and I so easily miss one of my two?"

"O, you must remember, that I have shot a good many more years than you have, for one thing. Why do you think you miss your second bird?"

"I suppose it is because they seem to be getting away from me so fast."

"Doubtless that is the root of the trouble. That was what prevented your killing the first bird, too, when you began to shoot, as you probably remember. When a flock of quail get up near a shooter, he has plenty of time to kill two birds, if he will only think so. The next time we put up a flock, stand and observe them, without shooting, and you will see how long the birds, or some of them, are within gunshot. I have found, too, that there are different kinds of wing-shots. Some men who shoot well in the open do not do nearly so well in the woods; and I hunted in Maryland once with a man who was a good shot, but who never even fired at the second bird when a flock got up. I used to advise him to carry a single-barrel gun. He said that when he was younger, he used to miss both birds often when the flock got up, and he reasoned it out that this was because he was in such a hurry to fire with both barrels. Accordingly, he would put in only one cartridge, and then he found that he had no trouble to kill the one bird."

Mose, who was a capital hand at marking the birds, told them just where the rest of this flock had gone, and they had an hour's fine sport. Mose was in luck, too, for he kicked an "old hare" out of the grass as he and Rob were walking along, which Rob shot, and his dinner was therefore assured.

Rob always found Mose very interesting, quite a different character from any of the colored people he had known in the North. He was a slave before the war, and could not read when he got his freedom. Mr. Bullis had taught him, and had given him a Bible of large print, and this elevated him to the distinction of preacher among his people. While they were having lunch at noon, near a brook, Rob made him the object of some of his questions.

"I hear you are a preacher, Mose. Do you get a good salary?"

"My people ain't got much salary to give. I depends mostly on collections. I preaches in de willage, and in two or tree oder places, and I makes out to keep de pot a bilin'."

"Mose is a farmer, too," said Mr. Bullis.

"Yes, I works a steer farm."

This, he explained to Rob, meant a farm just big enough to be worked with one steer. Some farms were called one-ox farms, and some team farms, the names designating the number of work-animals used on each.

"Dat steer of mine is de finest animal in dese parts," said Mose. "He can trabble, he can. When I goes to de camp-meetin' he trabbles eighteen miles an hour."

Mr. Bullis explained to Rob afterward that Mose meant to be truthful, but that his miles were a little short. Their number was all right.

"I never heard you preach," said Mr. Warren, "but I am told that you are a great preacher."

"Well," said Mose, by no means modest, "I was a preachin' at de willage one fall when some Nordern gemmen was here, and dey said dey heard me mos' two mile."

Mose evidently measured eloquence by sound.

Luncheon finished, Mose led the way again, and

then it was discovered that Mr. Bullis's dog Joe had disappeared. Calls and whistles did not bring him to them, and his master finally declared there was only one explanation of this, and that was that he had found birds and was pointing them. "And, if he is," said he, "he will stay with them till they get up themselves, if he starves to death." The party therefore divided to look for the dog, as there was not the slightest intimation of the direction he had taken. When Rob and Mose, who walked together, had mounted a little elevation, giving them a view of a pretty large cotton-field, Mose cried out, "De ole man was right. Dere's Joe sure enough, pointin', right in de middle of that cotton-field." He had probably been there for some time, but he showed not the first inclination to break his point.

Shouting for the others to come up, when the word "Hie on" was given, more than a dozen quail took flight. Three of them fell at the sound of the guns, Mr. Warren missing with his second barrel and Mr. Bullis and Rob only firing with their right. Rob experimented by aiming without firing his second barrel, and he told his cousin afterward that he found that he had time to cover two other birds.

The flock was followed up with fair success, and then Mose guided them to other ground.

As they were on the route for home about dusk, Cap pointed, and Rob, who was some distance from the others, put up the birds and fired at two. To his disappointment neither of them fell. Mose was ready to excuse the misses on account of the bad light, but Rob told him that he had a clear view of the birds and was never cooler in aiming. They decided to follow up these birds for one more shot, dark as it was growing. The field was a large one, dipping downward to a branch on the far side, and when this little declivity was reached, Cap pointed. "Now," said Mose, "you just go round the dog, and that will fetch the bird between you and the sunset, when you put it up, and you can see better to shoot it." Rob thought this a very good scheme, and he walked round Cap, and then approached him in the direction he was pointing. No bird arose, but Cap made a little spring forward, and picked up one of the birds at which Rob had shot. Delivering this to Rob, he ran on about fifty feet and pointed again, and, when Rob again walked up to him, he picked up a second dead bird.

Rob congratulated himself not only on securing two birds which had flown so far after being hard hit, but on the vindication of his aim. Mose told him that his experience was that a great many birds got away after being hit, and he recalled the story of a young man from the North with whom he had been out some years previously. The visitor was a poor shot, and he hunted with two companions who shot very well. But he had a slow dog which was a good retriever, and, after making a pretty clear record of misses in the forenoon, and, having several wounded birds, hit by the others, brought to him by his dog, he held back in the afternoon, and marked birds that the others fired at and did not drop, and, following them up, went in at night with a bag of six, only one of which he had shot himself.

Mose had led them a long tramp by the time they got home, but Rob declared that he had never enjoyed a day more, and he thought that a week in North Carolina every fall would make him a pretty good quail-shot. Mr. Bullis had more invitations for them from his friends, owners of plantations in different parts of the county, than they could accept, and on the remaining days of their visit they drove

Cap Delivering a Retrieved Quail.

QUAIL-SHOOTING IN NORTH CAROLINA

for some distance to their shooting-grounds. Everywhere they found the most open hospitality, and it was sometimes difficult for them to refuse the pressing invitation to spend the night. Mose always accompanied them, and, while he was not so well acquainted with the distant territory as he was with that nearer home, his "bird-instinct" was always good, and his assistance in marking the birds was invaluable. Rob felt, when they started for home, that he had made a good many friends, and they had to promise that nothing but necessity would prevent their repeating the visit the next autumn.

CHAPTER X

IN THE CANADA BUSH

ONE of Mr. Warren's acquaintances, who had been deer-hunting in Canada, gave him such glowing accounts of the deer there, that Mr. Warren thought that the discomforts of the trip, which were not concealed, would be outweighed by the novelty of the experience, and the quality of the sport. The result of much discussion of the subject between him and Rob, who at his age cared nothing about prospective discomforts, was a decision to make the journey. As the French Canadian at whose house they would stop lived many miles from the post-office, and visited it only occasionally, Mr. Warren was advised by his acquaintance to begin his correspondence about the expedition in plenty of time, and he accordingly wrote in September, asking Mr. Lebeau if they could be accommodated, and if he would make all the necessary preparations as regards dogs and boats. An answer came after

IN THE CANADA BUSH

a while, telling them to come, and promising to have everything in readiness and to give them some excellent shooting.

Accordingly, a November afternoon found our sportsmen landing at Kingston, Ontario, from the boat that had conveyed them from Cape Vincent, New York. They were now on foreign soil, and had a custom-house first to deal with. As each of them had a gun and a rifle, they were required to make a deposit on these, which would be returned when they came back to the city and departed again for the States. Their trunks, of which they had two small ones, were not opened, the officers taking their word that they contained nothing dutiable.

Learning that their train would not start until about four o'clock, they spent the intervening time making purchases of such stores as they thought they should need, and looking over the town. Their shopping was not so successful as it would have been had they arrived on a "market day." They were informed that the country people had a stated day, or days, for bringing in their produce, and, as they had not arrived on one of these days, they could get neither eggs nor butter. If they had known what was ahead of them they would have been more liberal purchasers, but they now satisfied themselves with some bacon, crackers, and sardines. If they had added to these coffee and a ham, their future larder would have been much more tempting.

Rob found Kingston on a cold and cloudy November day about as gloomy a place as he had ever seen, its gray stone houses adding to its sombre appearance, and a short drill by the red-coated troops at the fort affording all there was to see in the way of entertainment.

The Kingston and Pembroke Railroad at that time did not rely very much on passenger traffic, its main business being the hauling of ore from iron mines, and lumber from the forest along its route. Passengers were not, therefore, looked out for with any special care. So our travellers found their train made up of one so-called passenger car, that would not have done duty as a smoker on any road they were acquainted with in the States, and a number of empty freight and platform cars, before and behind it. Soon after they started it began to rain, and as their route was through an utterly uninteresting wooded country, the trip lacked every element of enjoyment.

After four hours of very slow travelling, and when it was quite dark, they came to the close of their journey for that day, a place called Mississippi (there is a Mississippi River in Canada, too), the end of that division of the railroad, where they would spend the night. A more desolate place could not be imagined, with a hotel of rough, unpainted boards, a hut for a station, and a few dwellings of the same character to constitute the settlement. But they had to make the best of the accommodations, and sat down, hungry, to a supper of cold fish, and poor bread and butter, and something called tea to wash it down with. Their company at table was half a dozen very rough-looking miners, who, they heard, would be guests of the hotel over night. When they were shown to their room, its two beds looked very uninviting, and there was no lock to the door. They made the best of the beds, however, and piled two chairs before the door as a precaution, and so passed the night with no other disturbance than that caused by some insect bedfellows.

After a breakfast, the most tempting feature of

which was some greasy fried pork-chops, they entered the cars again to complete their railroad journey. At the depot they discovered that their box of supplies purchased at Kingston had been left behind, and it did not reach them for three days. Less than an hour's ride brought them to the place where Mr. Lebeau's wagon was to meet them, but no wagon was to be seen. The only houses there were a rough shanty, which they learned was a loggers' boarding-house, when there were any boarders, a little store kept by a Scotchman, and the depot. The station-agent said that he knew Lebeau, but that his place was some fifteen miles distant, and that his wagon need not be looked for for some hours to come. Of course there was nothing to do but to wait.

The morning passed without the approach of a single vehicle to the settlement. At noon a team was seen advancing down the road and our travellers' hearts were cheered, but it proved to belong to an Irish settler, who was driving to the depot for some freight. He was of an encouraging disposition, and assured them of his belief that their host would send for them if he had promised to do so.

Before he left, an arrangement was made with him that, if the expected conveyance did not arrive by one o'clock, he would take them to their destination. To spend the night where they were was not to be thought of. A little before one o'clock another wagon drove up. The travellers did not think that this could be Lebeau's, as it had no seat, the driver sitting on the springless bottom on his horse-blankets. But they were mistaken. This was to convey them to their stopping-place. The driver, who had been hired to come for them, proved to be a surly fellow, and the only information they could obtain from him about the time of their departure was that it would be after he had fed his horses and himself. He went to the boarding-house for his meal, and Mr. Warren and Rob made a call on the Scotchman, and stayed their stomachs on some of his crackers and cheese.

When they were ready to start, and the driver was asked where his seat was, he replied that he could "borrow a board." And, indeed, had they had no trunks, an unplaned board laid lengthwise would have been their only seat for a long, rough ride. But the trunks were flat-topped, fortunately, and, with a horse-blanket for a cover, they made a fairly comfortable, if backless, seat. Their route lay through a featureless country, most of it still " bush," as the native forest is there called. There seemed no reason to doubt the driver's assertion that there were plenty of deer, since there were few houses, and they passed through only one small settlement.

About five o'clock, as they came in sight of a house, the driver announced that this was Lebeau's. It was the best-looking dwelling they had seen that day. Built of squared logs, it was plastered inside and out, and contained ten rooms in all, Mr. Lebeau having five sons at home to provide with lodgings. The old gentleman, who spoke with a decided French accent, gave them a warm welcome, and soon had their trunks unloaded, and escorted them to their rooms. Of the latter it may be said that they were small but comfortable, and that, while the mattresses on the beds were of straw, the beds were clean and the covers were abundant. They told him of their long fast, and supper was promised as soon as Mrs. Lebeau could prepare it. This supper proved a trial to Rob. It consisted of a big yellow dish containing fat side-pork, salt, swimming in its grease, potatoes, bread and butter and tea. Hungry as he was, Rob could not dispose of his piece of pork, and he had to make out on potatoes and bread and butter.

The little dining-room and the uncarpeted sitting-room adjoining were both warmed with the same stove, which sat in an opening in the partition between them. A number of loggers arrived by evening, on their way to a lumber-camp, so that every chair in the sitting-room was occupied. The evening was cold and the stove was kept almost red, in order to perform the double duty required of it, and every man smoked a pipe. Although Rob did not smoke, he had thought he was smoke-proof, but the air of that room soon got too thick for him, and he stepped to the door for a breath of purer atmosphere. "Leave the door open, lad," said Mr. Lebeau, " the boys do keep up pretty good fires in their pipes." Thus was set the programme for the evening: first, the room made dense with the smoke, and hot, then the opened door, till it became too cold for comfort, and then a filling up again with smoke.

Mr. Lebeau had a disappointment for them at the start. He confessed that his boys did not own a canoe, and had only one deer-hound, and that was lame. He had engaged a man from near the station, who owned a good canoe and several hounds (the one who had hunted with Mr. Warren's friend), to accompany the new-comers; but there had been a dispute between him and one of the Lebeau boys, and he had not kept his engagement. What were they to do? He thought they would better send one of the boys the next morning to try to buy a canoe, and he assured them that the deer were so thick that they would be certain to kill some on runways.

As we know, Mr. Warren did not kill deer by rowing up to them in the water, when he was out for sport; but he saw that venison must be their only dependence for fresh meat, and that their hound output was poor. So he decided to let the son go for a canoe.

The next day was Sunday, and the visitors spent it in taking a tramp with the eldest Lebeau lad as guide. This son's name was Elijah, but the family all called him Lujer. He was a good-natured fellow,

IN THE CANADA BUSH

possessed of a good deal of wood craft, and a pair of legs that seemed incapable of tiring, as they found before their stay was over. He blamed his father for not making better preparations for his guests, but said that his younger brother owned a collie that was a good deer-tracker as long as it did not tire out, explaining that he always ran with it to keep up its ambition. With this dog and his own hound he promised to get them some shots at deer without fail. In their walk they did rouse a deer from the bush, but they only heard it, the dense growth beneath the trees cutting off all the view.

It grew very cold that night, and when Rob awoke on Monday morning the glass in his window was thick with frost. Pat, the son who had gone to secure a canoe, and who had been allowed to carry Rob's rifle, had not returned, and his mother was loud in her lamentations, declaring that he had been drowned in crossing a lake. Mr. Lebeau was very comforting in his assurances that they could get a deer at the "pine-stump runway," a location near which he had killed one some ten years previously, and after breakfast (of salt pork in the yellow dish) the two set out, with Lujer as guide. A walk of two miles brought them to a big opening, known there as a *brûlé*—a burned space—the track of a forest fire of many years previous, studded with blackened stumps and logs, and grown up with weeds and grass. These *brûlés* are favorite feeding-places for deer, and Lujer hoped to start one there or in a swamp of evergreens just beyond.

The collie would stay behind them, but the hound had to be led by a strap until the hunting-ground was reached. When they arrived in the middle of this *brûlé*, which was cut up into ridges and hollows, the hound became very uneasy, and, tugging at the strap, slipped the collar over its head, and away it went. This was not according to Lujer's notion, and, laying down the shotgun which he carried, he started over logs and stumps after the dog. When he arrived at the top of the ridge in front of him, they saw him wave his arms and he called, "Hurry up here, hurry as fast as you can." Mr. Warren and Rob obeyed to the best of their ability, but when they arrived where Lujer was standing, nothing was to be seen. "What was it?" they asked. "O," said he, "when I got here a big buck was standing right by that old stump below there. You could have shot it sure." The hound had scented the buck, and buck and hound had disappeared in the before-mentioned swamp.

Lujer explained that he had intended to place the hunters on two runways before letting loose the dog, and now he feared the deer would not come near them. As they spoke, the dog was giving tongue, and lo, out of the swamp, half a mile ahead of them, came one deer after another, until six of the beautiful animals were in sight loping up a declivity, and disappearing in the bush. Lujer leaped up and down and howled out his disappointment, while Mr. Warren and Rob consoled themselves with the sight of six deer at once, waving their "flags," as their tails are called by sportsmen, and affording so rare a sight. Both declared that this exhibition in itself was worth the walk, but Rob did regret missing the chance of a shot, and Lujer was not to be consoled.

After a consultation, Lujer said that he would place the hunters on two good runways, and would try to get ahead of these deer, as he did not think they had gone very far, not having been shot at. "But how about the hound?" asked Mr. Warren.

"O," said Lujer, "he'll get tired." Perhaps this was comforting. As there was nothing better to propose, Lujer was allowed to carry out his plan.

Mr. Warren was placed on a ridge, out in the *brûlé*, near the place where the deer broke cover, and Rob was told to conceal himself in a clump of trees, which commanded a view of a little valley running off to the woods on the left. Then Lujer, with the collie, plunged into the brush. It was a long wait. Rob found it very chilly, standing where the wind had full sweep, and was compelled, after a time, to make himself more comfortable by crouching down behind a big rock. More than an hour after Lujer had left them, as he sat there, he thought he heard a cracking of branches in the woods below him. He tried hard to distinguish something in the dense growth, but in vain, although every now and then the sound would reach him, as if some animal was moving about. It might be the hound, he knew, and it might be Lujer. He hoped it was a deer, and that it would come his way. As Pat, the son who had gone for a canoe, had his rifle, he was armed with his ten-bore duck-gun, loaded with buck-shot, and he felt no doubt of his ability to bring down any deer that came within reasonable distance.

Then the sound ceased for some time, and he concluded that the animal, whatever it was, had gone, when right in front of him came the sharp bark of the collie, and out of the bush ran a beautiful yearling buck. As he learned afterward, this buck was not of the number of those that they had first seen, but had moved out of the bush, where it had passed the night, of its own accord, and the collie had crossed its trail and turned it as Lujer was returning from a futile attempt to head off the herd of deer.

The collie was a slow runner, and the buck took a moderate pace, directing its course toward the swamp out of which the other deer had been started. But instead of entering this swamp, it turned again, and ran through a hollow that brought it between Mr. Warren and Rob, too far for the latter to reach it with buckshot, but within fair rifle range of his cousin. Now, to shoot a running deer with a rifle, even if it is not going at full speed, is easier to be described by story-writers, whose heroes are the marksmen, than to accomplish in fact; and this is not a story of fiction. It must be admitted, therefore, that at the first shot of Mr. Warren the deer received no injury; the crack of the rifle did not even accelerate its speed. Again he fired, and again the deer escaped. But now it came to a place where the fallen logs were thicker, and where it was necessary for it to make a higher and a shorter leap, and when the rifle cracked a third time, down went the buck.

Lujer, who had kept in the bush meanwhile, but had watched the proceedings with interest, gave one of his shouts, and was by the deer almost as soon as Mr. Warren. The necessary dressing was accomplished by him in a few moments, and, with the buck across his shoulders, the party turned their steps homeward, well satisfied with the morning's result.

And what a supper that night! Out of the tenderest part of the back, Mr. Warren cut a pile of chops that was big enough to feed a dozen men at home, and, presiding at the stove himself, with the aid of a wire-broiler he produced a dish that would have tempted any good liver, even if he had not been sitting before stewed side-pork for two days. The question of meat supply was solved.

IN THE CANADA BUSH

Pat returned that night, in a snow-storm, without any canoe. He had been unable to buy one, and Mr. Warren had his doubts if he had gotten farther than the first public-house.

It snowed all night, but cleared off in the morning, and Lujer expressed great confidence in his ability to get Rob a shot by tracking in the snow. So he and Rob started out to take one course, while Mr. Warren, guided by Pat, was to take another, the two parties to meet at a designated point.

Lujer directed his course in the same direction as on the previous day, but, before reaching the *brûlé*, plunged into a low-lying growth of evergreens. His judgment in so doing was questionable, since the woods were so thick that, if he had started a deer, as he was quite likely to do, they would probably not have gotten a shot. The walking, too, was terrible, soft under foot, and with the snow sifting down their backs from the thickly laden branches. Lujer himself soon got enough of this, and, breaking out of the woods, led the way to an open, hilly district, where there was some chance of seeing a track on the ground.

And tracks soon appeared. There were unquestionably a great many deer in that country, and three had passed across an opening that morning. Rob wore over his trousers a pair of canvas overalls, that made a grating noise as he walked, and Lujer advised him to take these off, to insure greater silence. This done, they advanced with caution to the crest of a ridge, when Lujer grasped Rob's shoulder and pulled him down. "Do you see them?" he asked, pointing to a little valley ahead of them. Rob did the best looking he was capable of, but no deer met his eye. "Three of them," whispered Lujer; "right by the big stump." But Rob's eyes were not adjusted to deer. In fact, notwithstanding the sight of the one he had seen as it ran in the Adirondacks, he looked for something a good deal bigger, and the little brown things standing so quietly two hundred yards beyond, escaped him. "Let me take your rifle and I'll get one sure," said Lujer, whose faith in his own ball-loaded shotgun never was large, and Rob handed over the weapon. The rifle cracked. Three deer, all does, ambled away. Two more shots rang out, but no deer took notice of them.

"You missed them all," said Rob.

"Not much," declared Lujer. "Come down there and I'll show you."

When they got to the place where the deer had stood, Lujer, by careful search, was able to show Rob one little speck of blood on the snow. This satisfied him that his bullet had gone into some vital spot, and he assured Rob that he would be able to run down the wounded deer in a short time. So he placed Rob by a big tree in the nearby woods, telling him he might get a shot at deer which he (Lujer) was liable to start, and promising not to leave him there longer than half an hour.

But one hour passed, and then a good part of another, and the boy was miserably cold. The snow was half-knee deep, and he was so anxious not to lose a possible shot that he did not like even to tramp around to get up his circulation. But his ambition yielded in time, and, gathering some dead evergreens, he applied a match to them, and in a few moments had a glowing fire. Then he heard a call, and, answering it, was soon joined by his cousin and Pat. They, too, had seen tracks, but they had not had a sight of a deer. When Pat was told where Lujer had gone, he declared that they would be fortunate if they saw him by night, as he was more determined than a hound when he got on track of a deer.

But Lujer reappeared while they were eating their lunch. He came empty-handed, vowing, however, that his deer had bled for miles, but being unable to keep up with her.

Then Mr. Warren made a proposition. It was that Lujer should return to the house for the dogs and put these out in the swamp from which the six deer had run the day before, while he and Rob, with Pat as director, would station themselves where they would be most likely to get a shot. To this Lujer agreed, and off they started. Rob expressed a liking for the top of the ridge over which the six deer had disappeared, and Pat agreed with him that that would be a likely place to get a shot. When they came to the *brûlé*, Rob said he would select his own place of concealment on the ridge, and Mr. Warren and Pat took their station out on the other side of the *brûlé* where they would command a little valley.

When Rob got to the top of his ridge he found that it dropped very precipitously on the far side, the valley beneath being narrow. He argued, therefore, that, if a deer took the course of the day before, the place for him to stand was near the top of this ridge, and he selected a position which gave him a view of the *brûlé* and the swamp. Breaking off a branch of pine, he swept a place free of snow for his feet, and, having a rock as a partial shelter from the wind, he was ready to await a sound of the dogs.

Lujer had some distance to go to the house, and when he got there he solaced himself with a little of the pork stew and some hot tea. Then he found it slower work to lead the old hound than to take his own natural gait; and so it happened that Rob waited a long time before anything occurred to interest him. At one time he was entertained by the calling of one of the big woodpeckers that he had seen in the Adirondacks, but it did not come within sight. He imagined different directions in which a deer might appear, and he took imaginary shots at it. And all the time he was very cold.

But at last he heard what they were waiting for, the baying of a hound. It came from the swamp, and Rob took position, ready to do his part.

When he could locate the direction of the hound's movements, he decided that it was going through the swamp lengthwise instead of approaching him, and his hopes were dampened. Finally the baying ceased entirely. But it was soon followed by the sharper barking of the collie, and then his hopes rose again. This barking took a direction to his right, but it, too, soon ceased. Thinking that the deer might turn and pass through the valley just behind him, Rob ascended the ridge and watched for some time both ways. But it was cold and windy there, and after a time his hope deserted him, and he went down again behind his rock.

Scarcely had he regained his old station when the barking of the collie reached his ears, coming from the valley behind him. Had he only remained on top of the ridge! But to go back might turn the deer away again. Now the collie seemed to be climbing up from the valley. There was a breaking of brush ahead. Something was making its way over the ridge. Another moment, and a magnificent doe broke cover and went bounding down toward the swamp in graceful leaps.

If Rob's gun had been loaded with buckshot then,

he would have had no fears for the result of his shot. Whether he could bring down the doe with the rifle as it leaped, was to him a more doubtful question. But the lad was pretty cool. Dropping on one knee, he aimed and fired. Too high or too low. The shot missed. But it was not wasted. The deer had been paying attention only to the dog in her rear, and the crack of the rifle, coming from some unknown source, puzzled her. To locate it, she paused a moment in her flight. A second sufficed for Rob to pump another cartridge into the rifle-chamber and to aim behind her fore shoulder, and with the sound her legs doubled under her and her flight was over.

The young sportsman was by her side in an instant, ready to repeat the shot if it was necessary, but it was not. The collie came up and sniffed at the deer, and then lay down, satisfied with his part of the work. Presently Lujer with Mr. Warren and Pat came in sight. "What luck?" shouted Lujer. "I *saw* a fine doe," replied Rob. "You don't mean to say you let her get away from you?" "Not so easy," called back Rob, "to bring down a running deer." But Rob's expression was not that of a boy who had missed, and Lujer hastened up, saying, "You can't fool me. You killed that deer."

Rob was warmly congratulated by all, and the two brothers soon had the carcass, which was too heavy for one of them to carry, swung up between two young trees, to stay there and freeze, until some-one from the house came for it with a sled.

Mr. Warren got a deer on the following day, and the next day proved an unlucky one for both. Rob was assured that he had done well enough, but the great object of his ambition was a big buck with horns, and Lujer, who had taken a great liking to him, was very anxious to see that ambition gratified. "If we had a boat on Mosquito Lake," he kept saying, "I would give you a shot at the biggest buck in these woods. I've put him up four times, and he always makes right for that water." But only one day of their stay remained.

As they were sitting around the fire the last evening but one, Lujer said to his father, "Do you think we could do anything with the old scow on Mosquito Lake?" His father was doubtful, saying that the scow had not been used since the summer before, and was then in a poor condition. After some further discussion, Lujer proposed that Pat take Rob and Mr. Warren to the lake the next morning, while he tried to start the big buck with the hound. If the boat was found useless they could take their stands where Pat should decide, with a bare hope that one of them would be where the deer would enter the water. And this was finally agreed upon.

The morning proved cold and cloudy. It was a three-mile walk to the lake, and Lujer was to give them plenty of time to station themselves before he struck out into the woods. The lake was some two miles long, narrowing in places to 500 yards. They found all the little bays along its shore covered with thin ice, and Pat said that a deer would not take to water in any of these. The boat lay about half-way up the lake, and a wreck of a boat it proved to be. It was not actually unsafe, but its thole-pins were rotten, and, heavy when new, it was much heavier now in its water-soaked condition. Pat declared himself at a loss to know what to advise, and Rob finally said that he would make a suggestion in his own behalf.

About a quarter of a mile from the lower shore

of the lake, he had noticed a rocky little island. It was not more than a hundred feet in diameter, wooded with pine-trees, and rising up quite abruptly. Rob proposed that Pat land him on this island, as it would command a possible shot if a deer took to water in that part of the lake which was not frozen over, while Pat and his cousin took their stand near the boat, with the idea of trying to use it if nothing better was to be done. All voted that this was at least sensible, if not very hopeful, and this plan was carried out.

Rob found his island a perfect place of concealment, and he soon had a standing-place cleared of snow, and a seat picked out on a fallen log, and was ready for a long wait, if that was necessary. He did put in a long hour, getting so cold meanwhile that he ventured to light a little fire. (Lujer had told him that a deer was not afraid of a fire in the woods.) Then in the distance came the now familiar voice of the old hound. It seemed far away, and would die down entirely, as the animal ran into some little valley in the forest, and become distinct again as it rose to the top of a ridge. There was no doubt that it was coming nearer the lake. At first Rob was hopeful. Then the direction of the sound changed, and he now felt sure that the deer would enter above where his cousin was stationed, if at all.

Presently a new sound caught his ear—the sound of oars. Stepping across the island where he could command a good view of the main body of water, he could distinguish the boat being propelled toward him. As the hound was still giving tongue, he was puzzled at this move. But on looking closer he saw something some distance ahead of the boat which he at first took to be a little bush. But the bush moved too. Could it be? Yes, without doubt. It was the antlered head of a big buck!

The animal had taken to the water far ahead of the hound, out of rifle shot of Mr. Warren, and he and Pat were trying to approach it in the boat.

With a good boat this would have been no difficult task, and Rob's first thought was that he would only see his cousin get the prize, for even Mr. Warren, with his aversion to killing deer out of a boat, would not have let this buck escape him. But as the pursuit continued, Rob observed that the boat did not gain on the deer. As he learned afterward, the thole-pins were so rotten that Pat dared not put much pressure on them (he and Mr. Warren being both men of good weight), and all they could do was to keep the deer swimming on, in the hope that it would pass near Rob's island.

When Rob found that he was likely to get a shot, he nerved himself for his greatest effort. The cover on the island concealed him completely, and he made up his mind that he would let the buck come so near that he would not only be sure to kill it, but would be in no danger of knocking off any part of its fine antlers. A grand sight it made for him, as the animal chose its course, and came with a steady swim into close view. Rob was rather surprised to find how little of the buck was visible above the water, very little indeed except its antlers and its tail.

Soon it was Pat's time to get excited. Seeing nothing of Rob as the deer approached the island, and not being able to gauge the distance well from the level of the water, he made up his mind that Rob did not see the deer at all, and, not accepting Mr. Warren's assurances to the contrary (for Mr. Warren did not doubt that Rob was alive to the situation), he stood up in the boat and cried, "O Rob, why don't you shoot? Why the d—l don't you shoot?" This advice rather disconcerted Rob. Relying on Pat's knowledge of deer in general, and of this lake in particular, he supposed that there was danger of the deer changing its course and not giving him so good a shot as he could then have. The deer was now about a hundred yards from him, and swimming directly toward him, so that the mark presented was only the front of its head. Aiming very carefully, he pressed the trigger, and saw the ball strike the water less than an inch above the buck's ear. This was not so bad a shot, but a hundred such shots would not secure him the buck.

The animal now swung to the left, toward the shore, and then made directly from him. It was his one chance now, as every second increased its distance. Changing his position a little, he placed one foot on a fallen log, rested his elbow on his knee, and fired at the water-line.

With the crack of the rifle the buck apparently disappeared.

Then what a shout went up from that boat! Pat was wild. To have killed the deer himself would have given him not much more satisfaction. He shouted and he danced, and Mr. Warren told him that if he did not become quiet he would have a hole in the bottom of the boat.

A second look showed Rob that the deer had not sunk, its tail marking its position. That tail Pat soon had hold of, and thus was the buck towed up to the island, whence, after Rob had got aboard, it was towed on to the shore. There presently Lujer joined them, to enjoy the victory and to tell them how he had done a good part of the running of the deer himself, when the discouraged old hound showed a disposition to go home.

So ended Rob's experience in the Canada bush. It was practical roughing, with cold and hard work, but that buck's head paid for everything.

CHAPTER XI

WILD-GOOSE SHOOTING IN DAKOTA

ONE of Mr. Warren's schoolmates, who had taken up his residence in Dakota, had written him several times, giving him a pressing invitation to make a visit to that State, and see what sport he could offer him. He told of the vast number of wild geese and ducks that passed over the district in the migratory season, and said that larger game could be had by going a little farther west. At last the invitation was accepted, with Rob included in it, and a bright October morning found our two sportsmen on a train on the Northern Pacific Railroad, due in Bismarck at noon.

When they had retired to their berths the evening before, they were travelling through Minnesota. On arising, they found themselves on the broad prairies. This part of the trip was very interesting to Rob, who found the scenery, while monotonous, attractive from its novelty. On either side, as far as the eye could reach, stretched the almost level prairie, now a dull brown, treeless, and apparently devoid of life. It was hard to realize how recently the buffaloes had roamed over the same ground in almost countless numbers, and the warlike Sioux had disputed the occupancy of the land with every white comer. The absence of trees was perhaps the most remarkable feature of the landscape to the Eastern visitor. Not a single one stood out on the prairie as a landmark, and, even at the small settlements that had grown up around the railroad stations, no tree was to be seen. Here and there, over the prairie, a "shack," as the first log cabin of the settler is called, could be noted, but these were far apart, and Rob thought of the lonely life of the occupants.

It was a dry year in Dakota, but in many a depression where the land was rolling were little bodies of water, and from most of these wild ducks flew up at the approach of the train, giving Rob a hope that game would not disappoint them. He watched constantly from his window in the hope that at least one buffalo or antelope would show itself, but he was disappointed. How complete had been the extermination of the buffalo he learned a little later, when he

WILD-GOOSE SHOOTING IN DAKOTA

was told that 146,000 of the hides had been shipped from the Bismarck district in 1881, 80,000 in 1882, only 223 in 1883, and not a hide since. For the price of the hides the noble animal had been practically exterminated!

Arriving at Bismarck about noon, they landed on the piazza of the hotel which then constituted the depot platform (this was some twenty years ago, before the division of the State), where Mr. Warren's friend gave them a Western greeting. This friend, whose name was Frank Aileen, was a jolly man, of rotund proportions and a laughing eye, whose hopefulness nothing vanquished, whose stock of stories was inexhaustible, and whose Dakota experiences were of unflagging interest to Rob. "Come right in and get a bite," said he, "and then we are off. We must be shooting geese before sunset." Rob had gone to bed pretty tired with his long journey from New York the night before, and had supposed that they would require at least a day of preparation for the trip when they arrived; but the preparations had all been made in advance. The meal ended, they went to their room to don their shooting clothes, and then stepped into a light two-seated wagon and started back in the direction from which they had come. Mr. Aileen explained that his outfit was waiting for them at a station ten miles to the east, from which they would make their actual start.

Arriving there, Rob saw what looked to him like a gypsy outfit. There was a big wagon, to which were hitched a pair of mules, and which was piled high with such necessary articles as a tent, a stove, boxes of provisions, and, on top of all, two crates containing half a dozen live wild geese, the use of which will be described later. Mr. Aileen explained to Rob that it was necessary to carry with them everything they would require, as they would not only find no public-houses of entertainment, but would be fortunate if they camped near a settler who would spare them a few dozen eggs and some butter, even their firewood being included in their supplies. When the cavalcade started, it was led by the hunters in the wagon they had ridden out in, followed by the mule team, and all accompanied by two boys on broncos, one of whom went along "for fun," and the other, named Tim, to make himself generally useful. One seat in the light wagon was occupied

WILD-GOOSE SHOOTING IN DAKOTA

by a very important member of the expedition, Joseph, the colored cook, and with the mule team rode two young men who were considered "old residents" of the State (they had lived there five years), and who were to take care of things generally and shoot when they had an opportunity.

Starting due south, their route lay over the prairie, which was there somewhat rolling, the road being only a black streak ahead of them, where settlers' wagons had worn a path through the sod and into the rich soil. Not a traveller met them, and, as Mr. Aileen remarked, if they did find birds, they would have the shooting to themselves. The only form of life they saw on the ground was one badger, sitting by its hole. Toward evening many flocks of geese appeared in the distance.

It was about sunset when Sam, whom they honored with the title of "head guide," announced that they had reached their camping-place. To Rob he explained that they had been travelling toward the Missouri River, and aiming for a district where there were big wheat-stubbles. Goose-shooting in Dakota was conducted on an entirely different principle from that adopted on the coast. The birds here passed the night and the middle of the day along the river, where they could drink, bathe, and obtain gravel for their crops. At sunrise and in the afternoon they directed their flight to the big wheat-fields, where they fed on the grain that was stacked, or that had dropped on the ground as it was being harvested. In the spring the geese fed on the young grain, and the farmers thought them a nuisance, and were glad to have hunters shoot them and scare them away. As Rob looked over the flat prairie he wondered how a hunter was to conceal himself from the geese, but he repressed his desire to ask any more questions.

There was a settler's shack near by, and Mr. Aileen called on the owner to ask if there was a place under cover where any of the party could sleep. He was told that the settler's family occupied all the space in their one room, but that they were welcome to lie in the stable. The stable—a thatch-covered hovel— proved entirely untempting, and they decided to camp in true Western style, under the stars. Rob was delighted with this arrangement, as it seemed to make him an actual pioneer. While Joseph was setting up his stove and getting supper, the others partly unloaded the wagon and got things ready for

WILD-GOOSE SHOOTING IN DAKOTA

the night. It was a bright, starlight night, cool but not cold, and, as they thought that their stay where they were might be a short one, the tent was not pitched. Some hay from a nearby stack was spread on the sod for a mattress, the wagon-tongue was raised to a horizontal position, and on it a blanket was hung to protect them from the wind that is always on the move over the prairies, and some blankets to spread over them completed their sleeping arrangements.

Joseph gave them ham and eggs for supper, and they soon after discovered one of the inconveniences of prairie life in Dakota. The settler told them that the water near his shack was too strong of alkali to be drinkable, and Tim, the "useful boy," was sent on his pony to a spring half a mile distant, with a jug, to obtain a better supply. Thus did Rob learn at the start of one of the privations that some settlers in our new country have to endure; but this, unlike many others, could be remedied. The evening was spent listening to stories of Western experience, told by Mr. Aileen and the two "old settlers," and at nine o'clock they were all warned to go sleep, as they must be up before sunrise to try for geese.

The novelty of his situation might have kept Rob long from slumber even if there had been no other cause. In the first place, a prairie sod, although it has some hay on it, is not an easy bed to a "tenderfoot," and, while the two guides scorned even the luxury of hay, and slumbered at once, simply rolled up in their blankets, Rob, as he described it, "bored through" his hay in trying to get an easy position, and found the sod very hard. Off to the east the horizon was aglow with a distant prairie fire, and he thought of the stories he had read of escapes from such conflagrations, and wondered if this fire might reach them. Then he became interested in listening to an owl that kept up a hooting. Finally, when he thought he was going to sleep in earnest, Mr. Aileen put in operation a snoring-machine which Rob was sure had never been equalled in power and variety. Beginning with some long-drawn whiffs, it changed to a series of prolonged groans, which always ended in a snort that partly aroused the sleeper, as if the limit of a safety-valve had been reached and the surplus steam had finally escaped. Then, without any demand for an encore, the programme was repeated. This concert lasted about half an hour, dis-

WILD-GOOSE SHOOTING IN DAKOTA

turbed by frequent kickings and pokings by Mr. Warren, with only temporary effect, after which it ceased, and then all the camp became quiet.

Rob was pulled out of bed, while it was still dark, by Tim, who announced breakfast, for which they were ready as soon as they had washed their faces and hands in some alkali water, which made their eyes and lips smart; there was no dressing to do, as they had slept in their clothes. Their late arrival the night before had prevented any attempt at shooting during the evening, and Mr. Aileen was anxious to begin their sport at once. He decided that he would take Rob with him for the morning attempt, and leave Mr. Warren to the guidance of Sam.

Breakfast was soon eaten, and off Rob and his companion started, in the dark. Both carried ten-gauge guns, and an abundance of shells in canvas bags, and Rob was also loaded with a pick, while his companion carried a shovel. Here was occasion for another question, but Rob restrained himself. A walk of a little more than half a mile brought them to what Mr. Aileen said looked like a promising wheat-stubble, and he left Rob with the guns while he did a little prospecting. On his return he said,

"We're in luck. I have found some old pits that will save us a lot of digging."

"I'll have to ask what a pit is for," said Rob.

"O, I forgot that prairie shooting is new to you. Your cousin told me you had made a good record on the bay, and I did not think to explain why we brought with us a pick and shovel. As you see, the prairie is entirely without cover, and our geese are naturally as wild as are wild geese elsewhere. So we have to devise some means of getting near enough to them to shoot. Crawling up to them on a treeless prairie would not do, and the cover of an occasional grain-stack would give but a few shots. Accordingly we have devised the plan of digging pits in the grain-stubble and hiding in them. We dig a pit about hip deep, and of circumference sufficient to allow a man to squat down in it. One of these T-shaped stools suffices as a seat, and, with our decoys in front of us, and our eyes on the level of the ground, we are out of sight of the birds until they are within gunshot."

"But I do not see any decoys," said Rob.

"You are looking for the big decoys they use on the bay. We get along with something less bulky."

Undoing a bag, he brought out a dozen flat decoys of tin, which, he explained, when set so that the flying birds would get a side view of them, answered very well, especially if there was a big flight. "In the crates you saw on the big wagon," he added, "are our live decoys. These belong to Sam and his brother. They have collected them by saving crippled birds and keeping their wings clipped. Hoppled to a stake on the ground, the live birds will call to the flying ones, and in this way they are a big help, as an addition to the tin decoys. I did not try to bring any of them with us this morning, as this is a sort of exploration hunt. If we find the geese are flying well over this course, we shall make better preparations for the afternoon shoot."

They had now come to the place where Mr. Aileen had discovered the old pits. A little cleaning out of the loose earth made them serviceable, and Rob was soon ensconced in one of them. It seemed to him that it must be a very foolish goose that would mistake one of the tin decoys for a real goose, but Mr. Aileen told him he must remember that the goose was not credited with a large supply of brains, and that a hungry goose seemed to pay attention only to its stomach.

As soon as it was daylight occasional flocks of the birds were seen winging their flight from the direction of the river, but the course of most of them was far to the west of the place where the two gunners were watching. While the wild goose most abundant on the Atlantic coast is the large Canada goose, the variety shot in the largest numbers on the northwestern prairies is the *Hutchinsii*, a smaller bird with the same plumage. In the spring the snow goose, of white plumage, is seen in large flocks, as it is also in California. All the birds which our sportsmen got were of the smaller Canada variety.

It was some time after sunrise before the first goose came to them. This was a single bird, which was ready for any kind of company, and which accordingly took a close look at the tin stools. Rob was told that he could have the shot, and he tumbled it to the ground without difficulty. They killed two more in the course of an hour, and then Mr. Aileen decided that they were out of the line of flight, and they took up their stools and returned to the camping-place. Sam and Mr. Warren had

Shooting Wild Geese in Dakota.

already arrived there, with a single goose, and the wagon was soon ready for the move.

They travelled southeastward for about six miles, when they came to a district where there was abundant wheat-stubble, and moreover a deserted shack, of which they took possession. Mr. Aileen explained that on account of drought the wheat harvest had been almost a failure that year, and the settlers had generally moved to some place on the railroad, where they could make a living during the winter. This shack was a log cabin, with a fireplace and a door, and one window without glass. But it was well roofed and large enough to accommodate their whole party. Joseph soon had his stove connected with the chimney, and, while he prepared dinner, the others went out to look over the ground.

At dinner Sam proposed that he and Rob match themselves against the two older sportsmen for the afternoon, and this was agreed to. Sam soon had the horses hitched to the lighter wagon, and with guns, pick, spade, and three of the live decoys in it, and one of the boys to bring back the team, off they started. Sam selected as their stopping-place the middle of a big wheat-field, where the ground was a little elevated, so that they could have a good view of the distant prairie, and any geese that came their way could have a good view of their stools. The prairie soil is soft, almost like a black mould, and it did not take the two long to get two pits dug to Sam's satisfaction, he using the pick and Rob throwing out the loose earth. Then Sam tied the three live decoys to stakes where he wanted them, placed some tin ones to look as natural as possible, and they got into the pits and squatted down on the stools. Sam, who never neglected any precaution, had a hat for himself and one for Rob, on top of which were fastened the neck and head of a wild goose, so that when they peered above the rim of the pit their heads looked like two geese moving around. The only trouble Rob had with his hat was that it was top heavy, and had an inclination to fall over his eyes when his gun went off.

Sam had made no mistake in selecting his shooting-ground. By three o'clock geese were to be seen in large numbers taking their flight from the direction of the river, and soon a good-sized bunch came within sight of their decoys. Their live birds at once began to honk, and the flock replied and, setting their wings, came stringing up to them. "Take the head birds," said Sam, and their four barrels sounded. Three birds struck the ground with a thud (Sam declared that two of them were Rob's), and the rest went on. Sam leaped out of his pit, and kicked some of the black earth over the dead birds lest they frighten any new-comers, and was then hidden again and ready for some more. The next bunch were suspicious and refused to accept the decoys' invitation to make them a call, but a larger flock soon followed, and these came in nicely. It was indeed exciting to see the big birds approaching so steadily, in a long line, apparently filling the air in front of the shooters. It was somewhat easier to judge their distance than Rob had first found it on the water, but he always waited for Sam to give the word to shoot. They stopped four geese out of this flock, and Sam declared that they had the older men beaten "for sure." There was much friendly rivalry between him and Mr. Aileen, and he was determined not to come out second best on this trip.

Until sunset there was rarely a space of fifteen

minutes in which flying geese were not in sight. Most of the flocks of course passed out of gunshot —had they not done so it would have required a caisson to keep them in ammunition—but they got shot after shot, and there were not too many misses. Rob became very cool in waiting for the birds, and often tried to bring down two with one barrel, but they always strung out in line, after the manner of their kind, and he did not once succeed. At dusk Sam started for the team to carry in their game, leaving Rob to get any late-comers that he might see. He had one flock all to himself, and downed two of them, and these brought their score up to twenty-nine birds. They almost filled the wagon-body; Mr. Warren and his companion had secured only eighteen. They did include in their bag a sand-hill crane, which Mr. Aileen contended should count for five geese, but Sam disallowed the claim.

Joseph gave them a great dinner that night, with roast goose as the centrepiece. Rob thought that he had never tasted anything more delicious than the breast of a young goose, even if it lacked the accompaniment of jelly and dressing that would have been provided at home. The evening was fine, and they gathered on the lee side of the shack, where the elders smoked and all listened to stories of hunting experiences. Mr. Aileen told of a bear-hunt he had indulged in, the first year he went West; how he had been stationed on the border of a thicket, as the most likely place for the bear to come out (any less likely place would have suited him much better); how the bear—a big cinnamon—did come out where it was expected to, not more than seventy-five yards from where he was sitting, frightening his pony so that it ran away, leaving him to engage with the bear on foot, and with not a tree within sight as a place of refuge.

"When I started out," said he, "I had no doubt that the rifle I carried could despatch a bear of any size within two hundred yards; but when that big bear—it looked to me bigger than a steer —came out of the bushes, my weapon felt like a popgun in my hands. I let that bear sit up and look at my fleeing horse, and at me, too, if I came within its range of vision, and I did not move a muscle. Shoot? No, sir. That bear had given me no intimation that it liked to be made a target of, and I did not propose to cross its feelings until hostilities became necessary. After completing its observation, it broke off and ate a few branches of berries and then it disappeared in the thicket again. I had saved my life. Now it was necessary to save my reputation. Going to the place where the bear had sat up, I carefully obliterated its tracks outside the thicket with a brush of berry stalks, and then resumed my vigil. Presently out came the two old hunters who had been beating the thicket. 'See the bear?' 'I heard something in the edge of the thicket, and my horse ran away.' They examined the thicket where the bear had disappeared, saw the tracks leading up to the edge opposite me and then turning off, and inquired if I had sat all the time where I had been placed. Then they grasped my hand and declared me 'a brave man' to be willing to face a cinnamon on foot, and without a place of refuge. Unwilling to destroy so pleasant a delusion, I said no more."

At turning-in time, hay from a nearby stack was carried into the shack, and a good thick bed made for all who wanted it. Mr. Warren then directed the boys to close the window and the door with some boards and blankets. "Close the window and the door?" said Mr. Aileen. "Conscience, man, we want air, not heat."

"Frank," replied Mr. Warren, "did you note how few birds we saw this morning?" Frank had noted. "And do you know how to account for their scarcity?" "Only that we were not on the line of flight." "No, my friend; *they* were on the line of sound. The goose is not hatched that will fly where the sound of your nose, when one of your night-concerts is under way, can reach. To-night we shall bottle up that sound, and to-morrow we shall kill more geese."

All slept later the next morning, and Rob, who was among the earliest risers, slipped away to an old pit he had noticed the afternoon before, while Joseph was getting breakfast, and had the luck to see a fine flock of geese light within a hundred yards of him and feed. He watched them with interest for some time, and at last, when he heard himself called to breakfast, threw a stone into the flock and so flushed them. They circled around, unwilling to leave their breakfast half-eaten, and then flew directly over three decoys he had put out, and he killed two of them.

As the morning flight did not seem to be heavy —they could see in all directions from the shack— Mr. Warren proposed to go with Rob to a tree-claim near by and show him some grouse. Mr. Aileen had explained to them that what were called prairie-chickens in Dakota differed from the more common prairie-chickens of Iowa and other of the States farther east, being a somewhat heavier bird, but similar in plumage. The prairie-chicken is the pinnated grouse (*Tympanuchus cupido*), while the common bird of the North Dakota prairies is the sharp tailgrouse (*Pediæcetes phasianellus*).

Rob had a question to ask as they walked along: " What was a tree-claim ? " He was told that, some years before, Congress, in order to induce the new settlers to attempt forest culture, passed a law granting title to government land in one way as follows: The settler could lay claim to a tract of 160 acres by " timber-culture entry." This done, he was required to break up the sod on five acres of this land the first year. The next year he must seed these five acres and break up five more. The third year he must plant the five acres first seeded with slips, or seeds that would produce trees, and go on

WILD-GOOSE SHOOTING IN DAKOTA

in this way until the whole tract was tree planted. It may be explained that this system did not prove satisfactory, and the tree-culture act was repealed some years ago.

A half-hour's walk brought them to one of these tree-claims. To Rob it looked like a big piece of land brushed for peas. The claimant had gone to the Missouri River bottom and secured small growths of cotton-wood, and set these out at proper distances. The "forest" was still young, but many of the slips were dead, and there seemed a poor chance of maturing any of them on land where it was in many years too dry to grow wheat. But the grouse took naturally to this kind of cover, and it was much easier to look for them in such a place than to try to flush them on the wide extent of prairie, where the grass was generally thin, and a dog (they had no dogs with them) might run his legs off before finding game.

They had advanced but a short distance in the claim, walking rather far apart in order to beat it as well as possible, when Rob flushed a grouse. It got up with heavy wing, giving out a harsh sort of cackle, and flew toward the open prairie. Rob kept his gun levelled at it so long that his cousin called out, "Why don't you shoot?" and then he fired and downed the bird. "It flew so easily," Rob explained, "that I wanted to take time to get a good look at it. I don't see how a man who can kill our ruffed grouse in the woods can find any excuse for missing these birds in the open." Mr. Warren agreed with him, and he said that on this account the prairie-chickens of the more Eastern States were almost exterminated, and the strictest laws were being enacted for their protection.

One more grouse was flushed in the tree-claim, which Mr. Warren killed. On a subsequent day, as they were walking ahead of the wagons, they saw six sitting on a haystack near a deserted shack, and got four of them by marking where they lighted in a piece of uncut corn.

Their stay on the prairie lasted a week, with some days that gave them big bags of geese and some that were disappointing. It is not necessary to count up the total number killed. But they did not kill simply for the sake of killing. A wagon that came out from Bismarck went back loaded with geese for their friends and to be put on ice, and more than one of the few settlers whose shacks were occupied received presents of birds as they drove along. There was much discussion of an expedition to the Northwest in search of deer and bear, but all accounts represented the country as dried up, and that sport was deferred to another year. The drought also cheated them of their expected duck-shooting, as all the big sloughs were now mere beds of alkali. They set out on their return to the East therefore with only geese to their score, but with recollections of a novel experience, and with promises of a much greater variety of sport if they would repeat the visit in a wet year.

Reprint Publishing

For People Who Go For Originals.

This book is a facsimile reprint of the original edition. The term refers to the facsimile with an original in size and design exactly matching simulation as photographic or scanned reproduction.

Facsimile editions offer us the chance to join in the library of historical, cultural and scientific history of mankind, and to rediscover.

The books of the facsimile edition may have marks, notations and other marginalia and pages with errors contained in the original volume. These traces of the past refers to the historical journey that has covered the book.

ISBN 978-3-95940-156-2

Facsimile reprint of the original edition
Copyright © 2015 Reprint Publishing
All rights reserved.

www.reprintpublishing.com

www.ingramcontent.com/pod-product-compliance
Lightning Source LLC
Chambersburg PA
CBHW050556170426
43201CB00011B/1718